Never to Be Forgotten

Never to Be Forgotten

A Young Girl's Holocaust Memoir

by
Beatrice Muchman

KTAV Publishing House, Inc.
Hoboken, New Jersey 1997

Library of Congress Cataloging-in-Publication Data

Muchman, Beatrice, 1933–
    Never to be forgotten : a young girl's Holocaust memoir / by Beatrice
Muchman.
        p.   cm.
        ISBN 0-88125-598-X
        1. Muchman, Beatrice, 1933– 2. Jewish children in the Holocaust—
Belgium—Biography. 3. Jews—Belgium—Biography. I. Title.
DS135.B43M83   1997
940.53'18'092—dc21   97-8828
                                                         CIP

Manufactured in the United States of America
KTAV Publishing House, 900 Jefferson Street, Hoboken NJ, 07030

This book is dedicated to my parents, Julius and Meta Westheimer, whose love and courage transcend time. To my son, Robbie, whose beloved memory I will cherish all the rest of my life. And to my treasured daughter, Wendy, so that she may preserve her legacy and tell the story.

CONTENTS

Of the 57,000 Jews who lived in Belgium at the time of the German occupation, 29,000 survived. Like all Belgian resisters, the members of the CDJ (The Jewish Defense Committee) paid a higher price than those they defended. Of its eight founding members, six were deported, and of those, only two survived.

Yvonne Jospa, a key figure in the Jewish Resistance, recalled "I was the head of the Jewish children's committee within the CDJ. Of the 4,000 children the CDJ placed more than 3,000 were saved."

Based on "The Rescuers"
by Gay Black and Malka Drucker

The suffering that exists here makes heaven cry!
—Walter Hurwitz, writing about conditions at an detention Camp Gurs in France, December, 1940.

You don't know it; no, you can't grasp the misery that was spared you. You are outside luck itself.
—Frieda Hurwitz, describing life in Belgium during the Nazi terror, in a letter to her sister, October, 1945.

I will keep you as a treasure, and later on, when my hands or the hands of my children open your pages . . . it will be a reminder to everyone about a little country far away called Belgium.
—Béatrice Westheimer, age thirteen, making the last entry in her Belgian journal, October, 1946.

In the beginning my accomplished student, Kathy Stamp, gave each letter that I translated a resting place by spending untold hours at her computer. In her capable hands the letters were categorized according to the years in which they were written and the family members who wrote them. Together, we worked to unravel a seemingly endless maze and arrived at a chronological list of letters that came alive to tell the tragic, yet inspiring story of a resilient family in search of one another and a path to safety in America.

Professor Henri Hurwitz, my cousin, is part of the story. He traveled far to help me decipher his own father's miniscule handwriting and translate his letters. Henri is the family historian—his recall and wealth of knowledge never cease to amaze me.

Maxime Steinberg, Belgian historian and the author of many valuable books on the Holocaust personally offered me the background and encouragement to write and publish. So did my rabbi, Donald Gluckman.

My agent, Muriel Nellis, took this project to her heart and worked diligently to try finding it a home. She introduced me to Paul Engleman, who became my editor. Paul is a Catholic of German ancestry, well qualified to work on the story of a German-Jewish girl who was once a Catholic convert. We became immediate friends. Without his literary talent and dedicated long evening hours, this book might still be in the making.

Although she lived long and wisely, Anita Muchman, my mother-in-law and loyal fan, did not live long enough to see this book in print. It would have held a place of honor in her extensive library.

Never too busy to answer my phone calls to her office at Encyclopaedia Britannica, or to her home, Marilyn Klein—copy editor, supervisor and dear friend—acted both as critic and fact finder whenever and whereever her schedule permitted.

More than a dozen good friends and an almost equal number of family members agreed to read early drafts of the manuscript. They managed to

ACKNOWLEDGMENTS

complement the book so skillfully that I hardly realized I was being corrected.

In the end, at KTAV, the very personable Bernard Scharfstein, his detail-minded editor, Robert Milch, and his talented and thoughtful book designer, Dorcas Gelabert, turned these pages into the real book, "Never To Be Forgotten."

To them all, I am deeply grateful.

But, most of all, for his enduring patience, vivid humor, love and support, I wish to thank Irwin Muchman — my husband and my best friend.

The first time I saw my father cry was the second-to-last time I saw him. I was nine years old. That was more than fifty years ago, during the summer of 1942.

We were in the Belgian countryside, in the town of Ottignies, about twenty-five kilometers from Brussels. My father had brought my cousin Henri and me there on a long train ride that morning. We were at the home of two Catholic women, where we were to spend the summer.

My father began weeping when he kissed me goodbye. The women, who were sisters, looked on awkwardly. Or maybe I was the one who felt awkward, wanting so much to look like a grownup and embarrassed to see my father, of all people, acting like a child.

I understood a lot of things by the time I was nine years old. After fleeing our home in Berlin and moving to Brussels three years earlier, after learning to speak French and, more importantly, not to speak German, after being forced to quit school and hide in our cramped apartment for fear of discovery by the authorities, I understood things that a child that age should not have to know—things that too many children my age, at that time, knew all too well.

But on that beautiful summer day I did not, or perhaps would not, understand why my father was crying.

My parents had prepared me for the trip, telling me I would enjoy life away from the city—the fresh air, the sunshine, the flowers, the trees. But the way my father was behaving, spending my summer in the country seemed like anything but a good thing. He was spoiling what was supposed to be a wonderful moment in my life.

It wasn't until much later that I came to realize why my father was crying. He knew deep inside that this very well might be the last time he would ever see his daughter, his only child. But he did not mention that to me, and I was too young to understand such a possibility.

He was gone in what seemed like an instant, rushing out the door, starting on the long walk down the steep hill leading back to the train station. I tried hard to put him out of my mind, as the two middle-aged sisters attempt-ed to make Henri and me feel at home in our new surroundings. But when I went to bed that night, I was still thinking about my father crying. I felt fright-ened and alone.

Despite all the things I understood back then, despite all my efforts to see things as a mature young lady, I only knew them through a child's eyes. When I was told a year later that my father had been shot to death by German soldiers, there was a part of me that didn't believe it, a part of me that didn't yet understand the finality of death. When I learned at the same time that my mother had been captured and taken away, I didn't dare believe that she was gone forever. I was sure I would see her again and I convinced myself it would be soon. I was wrong, of course, but having that belief to cling to made it possible for me to cope and survive during a time of great personal anguish.

I've carried the memories from that period of my life for more than half a century now, and at many times they have been an oppressive burden. But there are also good memories from that period, of people whom I came to cherish for the rest of my life, people who were willing to risk their lives to save mine. My parents, of course, made the ultimate sacrifice—giving me up, their only child. But being a child, I had no understanding of what an agonizing decision that was for them. Not until years later, when I had my own children, did I begin to appreciate it. But at the time, and in the years following, it was hard to overcome the feeling that my parents had not saved me, but abandoned me.

Like so many other people who lost loved ones during the Holocaust, I learned very little about what happened to my parents. Most of what I knew came from my grandmother and aunt immediately after the war. Some forty years later their account was validated for me in Volume II of Belgian histo-rian Maxime Steinberg's, *La Traque des Juifs, 1942–1944*. My parents were among a mass of deportees—on a transport to Auschwitz—who attempted a unique escape. Despite the dispassionate rendering, in which my mother and father were mere numbers on a transport, reading about them on a printed page somehow made their lives—and their deaths—more real for me.

Some years later, my daughter, Wendy, made a discovery that had a far greater impact on me than reading about my parents in Steinberg's book. It was a discovery that brought my memories of them and that period of my life into a much sharper focus. More important, it changed my life at a time when I was recovering from another personal tragedy—the death of my son in a senseless car accident.

Wendy made the discovery at the home of my adoptive father, Werner Lewy, the uncle with whom I had gone to live in Chicago after the war. Werner had died, and Wendy was helping my husband and me close his estate and dispose of his personal effects. We had completed most of the job, and on this particular day Wendy was there alone, sifting through stacks of dusty boxes on overhead shelves in a bedroom closet. The last box that Wendy found aroused her curiosity. Unlike the other boxes, it was taped shut. Inside she found a black three-ring notebook bulging with brittle yellowed papers. They were mostly faded letters, handwritten on odd-sized sheets of stationery, but among the letters there also were official-looking documents and old photographs.

Most of the letters and documents were in German, a few were in French and English. From glancing at the dates, Wendy could see that they had been written during the 1940s. Names of relatives whom she had heard about but never met leaped at her from the lines. Two names in particular stood out: Julius and Meta Westheimer. My mother and father.

Wendy was reluctant to tell me about her discovery. She was afraid it would upset me too much. A few years earlier, her brother, Robbie, my only son, had been killed by a drunk driver, and she wanted to spare me further heartache. But she soon realized that for me the value of the information in the letters would outweigh whatever sad memories they brought.

The experience of poring over the contents of that box, of seeing my mother's handwriting again after so many years and reading about the agony that the adults around me were going through during that period of time, was indeed devastating. At first I was angry that my uncle had never shared the contents of the box with me during the forty-five years we both lived in Chicago. It was inconceivable that he had forgotten about them, being a person who was committed in the later years of his life to keeping memories of the Holocaust alive. Had he needed to protect himself from the painful memories, or had he been trying to protect me?

I'll never have the satisfaction of knowing the answer to this question, but the letters themselves provided many answers to questions that I had put aside long ago, as well as to new ones that arose. Like the pieces of a lost puzzle, distant dates, lives, and events came together for me in a new and clearer light. During the many months that I sat up late into the night, deciphering, decoding, and translating the tiny scribbled words crammed onto every inch of precious brittle yellowed scraps, the letters reminded me of all that I had seen and enabled me to see how much I had missed. They brought to life beloved human beings I had known as a child and others I had barely known. My mother and father once again became real and close—people I could touch and understand.

Rekindling memories that had smoldered for so many years, the letters also prompted me to go back through a diary that I had kept as a child, enabling me to compare what I observed and felt with what I had chosen to record. The neat handwriting and carefully selected words revealed how well I was able to hide my real feelings. The way I wrote is how I coped— by trying to be the perfect child, the happiest child, to please everyone around me so that I would deserve their care.

Presenting the letters and my diary and writing about these years seemed at first a way of giving my parents and the events that surrounded their tragic deaths a place to rest. It was also a way to keep their spirit clearly remembered for my daughter and any children that she may have. But it soon became much more than that. It became a deeply personal and troubling journey to my past, bringing back the fear and pain I felt as a little girl abandoned by her parents. As a child, I had not grasped the terrible circumstances and agonizing choices that my parents faced. In making the courageous decision to give up their only child and hide her from the Nazis, they also had been forced to keep me hidden from seeing their love.

More than half a century later, through the good fortune of discovering their letters and reading about how I had filled them with joy and pride, I finally was able to discover, in a deep, fundamental way, that my parents had loved me more than life itself. Translating their letters and writing about those years became my chance to forgive them and embrace them and thank them.

BOAS FAMILY CHART

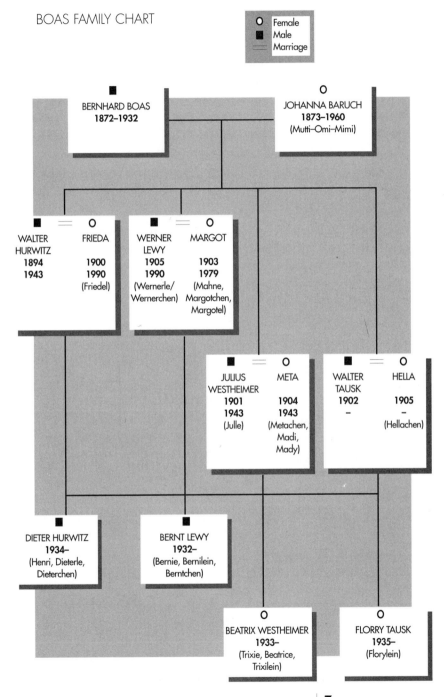

	Female
	Male
	Marriage

BERNHARD BOAS
1872–1932

JOHANNA BARUCH
1873–1960
(Mutti–Omi–Mimi)

WALTER HURWITZ
1894
1943

FRIEDA
1900
1990
(Friedel)

WERNER LEWY
1905
1990
(Wernerle/ Wernerchen)

MARGOT
1903
1979
(Mahne, Margotchen, Margotel)

JULIUS WESTHEIMER
1901
1943
(Julle)

META
1904
1943
(Metachen, Madi, Mady)

WALTER TAUSK
1902
–

HELLA
1905
–
(Hellachen)

DIETER HURWITZ
1934–
(Henri, Dieterle, Dieterchen)

BERNT LEWY
1932–
(Bernie, Bernilein, Berntchen)

BEATRIX WESTHEIMER
1933–
(Trixie, Beatrice, Trixilein)

FLORRY TAUSK
1935–
(Florylein)

THE BOAS SISTERS

FRIEDA (Friedel): 1900–1990
Business woman, bookkeeper. Most intellectual of the sisters. Studied voice (opera). Marriage arranged by parents to attorney Walter Hurwitz. Emigrated from Berlin to Brussels in 1937.
Child: Dieter (Henri)

MARGOT (Margotel, Margotchen, Mahne): 1903–1979
Bookkeeper. Studied violin and piano. Headstrong, fun-loving; talented in cabaret improvisations. Married Werner Lewy, ambitious salesman and businessman. Emigrated to United States in 1940.
Child: Bernt (Berni, Bernilein)

META (Madi, Mady, Metachen): 1904–1943
Commercial artist, fashion designer, poet. Most creative of the four sisters; wished to become ballerina. Married entrepreneur Julius (Julle) Westheimer, athlete and champion oarsman.
Child: Beatrice (Beatrix, Trixi, Trixie, Trixilein)

HELLA (Hellachen): 1906–
Youngest of the sisters, the baby of the family. Married Walter Tausk, business man and amateur boxer. First of the sisters to emigrate to United States.
Child: Flory (Florylein)

I was born in Berlin in 1933, the year Hitler came to power and a chaotic year in the lives of my parents, Julius and Meta Westheimer. The political situation was already uncomfortable for Jews and would become increasingly so over the next few years, as their rights were steadily and relentlessly stripped away. Although I have few memories prior to fleeing the city when I was five years old, I can recall having a strong feeling, even as young child, that something was very wrong in my world. Undoubtedly this came from listening in on anxious conversations between my parents and other relatives and sensing the rising tension in our house.

My father was an orphan. My mother had three sisters, Frieda, Margot, and Hella, all of whom were married. Their mother, Johanna Baruch Boas, was the oldest of several children. Her daughters called her Mutti, a German endearment for mother. To most of her grandchildren she was known as Omi, an endearment for grandmother. I always called her Mimi. She and everyone else in the family called me Trixi.

Mimi and her husband, who died in 1932, had owned a small Publishing House. Under their vigilant tutelage, their four daughters all became self-sufficient. After my grandfather died, Mimi's brother, Richard Baruch, took over the role of family patriarch.

Uncle Richard and his wife did not have any children of their own. He was the wealthy owner of a department store in Berlin. My earliest memories are of gathering with the family on Jewish holidays and special occasions at their beautiful, spacious apartment. I remember that Uncle Richard would splatter me with wet kisses as soon as we arrived. Mimi would be my savior, swooping in to rescue me. That was probably the first of the many reasons I came to love her so dearly.

Petite, quick-witted, energetic, and at times authoritarian, my grandmother reigned supreme at family celebrations. She was the hub of the family and held great influence over her daughters, especially my mother, according to what I later learned from relatives.

Knowing what we have come to know, it is difficult to understand why the members of my family chose to remain in Berlin until the hostility toward them became absolutely unbearable and their options had disappeared. But as contributing citizens in a country where their ancestors had served prominently in the military, they considered Berlin their rightful home. My father had a good job as a salesman, and my mother was a successful fashion designer. Like Mimi, Uncle Richard, and some of their friends, they underestimated Hitler, believing that his popularity would be relatively short-lived.

My mother's youngest and oldest sisters, Hella and Frieda, saw the handwriting on the wall and left Germany before we did. Hella and her husband, Walter Tausk, emigrated to New York in 1936 with their daughter, Flory. The following year Frieda and her husband, Walter Hurwitz, an attorney who, as a Jew, had already been banned from practicing law, emigrated to Belgium with their son, Dieter, whom we all came to call by his French name, Henri.

For my father and mother, her sister Margot, and Margot's husband, Werner Lewy, the urgency of leaving Germany finally became clear on November 9, 1938, the night of terror that came to be known as Kristallnacht. It is also my first really vivid memory from childhood.

I woke up to the sounds of people shouting and glass shattering down in the street. I could see flames at my bedroom window and thought that the drapes were on fire. When I cried out, frightened and confused, my father rushed into my room and picked me up. With my mother beside him, he carried me down the stairs to the street. There was trash and broken glass everywhere. People were running and shouting. I felt cold and frightened, and tried to keep warm by clinging to my father's chest.

I remember my father looking terrified as he told my mother that the

Nazis were burning the synagogues. The flames I had seen out my window were from our synagogue, a block away. I didn't comprehend the significance of synagogues being destroyed, but I could sense my parents' panic, and it frightened me. Seeing the fear on their faces made me realize that something terrible was happening.

The family gathered together several times over the next few weeks. I did not know what they were talking about, but I could sense the urgency of their meetings. Four months later, in March, 1939, seven of us set off for Brussels—Aunt Margot, Uncle Werner, and their son, Bernt; my parents, Mimi and I. We were accompanied by two strangers whom my father and uncle had hired as guides. Mimi later told me they were dishonest men who had charged a lot of money and done little to assist our escape. In the frantic days after they had been hired, the adults in my family were fearful that the men would keep the money and report my father and uncle to the authorities. On our long trek to the Belgian border, there was fear that the men would abandon us in the woods.

We left the city in absolute secrecy. I'm not sure that Mimi, who at sixty-five was leaving her whole life behind, even took the risk of telling her exact plans to her brothers and sisters. Because we had to hike so far through the woods, we packed almost nothing. We wore as many of our clothes as we could put on.

We must have started out in a car or on a tram, but I have no recollection of that. In my mind it is as if I were transported from the blinding fire at my window to the blinding darkness of the forest. The journey probably lasted two days, but in my memory it is one long terrifying night.

Sometimes we walked, sometimes we crawled. My biggest fear was being caught by guard dogs. Even while riding on my father's shoulders, a spot as safe and secure as any I could imagine, I was deathly afraid that one of the dogs would catch me. I didn't understand who these strange men were or why the adults were relying on them. Sensing my parents' distrust, I too felt afraid of them.

Having to remain silent, not being permitted to speak—that was the hardest thing for me. But my parents had prepared me well. I believed that if I spoke, a dog would find me and attack me. As much as a young child understands what it means to be killed, I understood that if we were caught, something terrible would happen. If I dared to speak we would be caught. For hours and hours and hours, I didn't say a word.

| **1939**

After the terror of our escape from Berlin, living in Belgium was a huge relief. The families of three of the Boas sisters—the Lewys, the Westheimers, and the Hurwitzes—were temporarily reunited. I remember it as a happy time and, compared with the recent situation in Berlin, it undoubtedly was.

Being a young child, I wasn't aware of the hardships we faced. My family arrived in Brussels with few possessions. Nobody spoke French well or Flemish at all. We were there on interim visas and there was no possibility for legal employment. But everyone remained hopeful. America was our ultimate destination, and in the meantime we had each other.

The Hurwitzes (Frieda, Walter, and Henri) had come to Brussels two years earlier and lived in Uccle, an affluent district on the edge of the city. We Westheimers and the Lewys settled in cramped but separate quarters in a modest three-story apartment building on *Chaussée de Wavre* in the center of the city. They lived in an attic apartment and we lived right below them.

My grandmother alternated, living with all three families in turn. Mimi was a matriarchal figure in those days, and her strong-willed ways added to the tension in each household. Even at so young an age, I could tell that she disapproved of my father and he did not like her. They hardly spoke to each other, and he was often in a bad mood when she was around. But for me, Mimi was a loving presence, not only my babysitter but a trusted confidante during the long days when my parents were out of the apartment struggling to earn a living.

During those early days in Brussels, I spent much of my time playing with my cousins. Bernt Lewy was a year older than I was, and Henri Hurwitz a year younger. The only girl in the middle of two boys, I remember myself as a little flirt, an assessment that the adults who survived would later confirm.

I also had an active imagination, owing mostly to my mother, who had it in mind that I someday would be a movie star. She was a beautiful woman; gentle, soft-spoken, and creative. In Berlin she had been a fashion designer and had arranged for me to be a photographer's model. In Brussels, I remember her sewing constantly. She made clothes for all of us seemingly from nothing, and the prettiest things were made for me. She would wrap my hair around thick wooden rollers to give me curls in the style of Shirley Temple. It was no coincidence that Shirley Temple was the person I most wanted to be. I was forever playing at being an actress, wandering off into a fantasy world whenever I wanted. During those tension-filled times, my world of make-believe was a warm refuge that my mother encouraged. This ability to let my imagination carry me away served me well throughout my childhood, especially later when I was separated from my family.

My father was a thin man, outwardly cheerful and optimistic, but he had a streak of stubbornness that probably had a lot to do with his having been an orphan as a child. Although old photographs show that he was taller than my mother, I remember it the other way around. Of course my recollection of his height might have been be affected by my uncle, Werner Lewy, who, at six feet three inches, towered over everyone—especially his wife, Margot, who was barely five feet tall.

My father was a salesman by trade, and despite his poor grasp of French, he soon managed to find work with a food company. At a time when food was scarce, this was an enviable position. Sometimes he would come home with a treat for me. I can recall watching for him late in the afternoon, with my face pressed to the window, wondering what he would have for me that night.

Despite their efforts to protect me, it was hard in that small apartment for my parents to keep me from sensing how difficult things were. They argued frequently, mostly out of frustration from trying to procure the necessary papers to arrange our departure from Belgium. Life was totally taken up with talk of getting visas.

In 1939, this was no easy task. The immigration laws were constantly changing. The United States was reluctant to accept immigrants in general and Jewish immigrants in particular. To secure a visa, an applicant had to have an affidavit from an American citizen certifying that he or she was willing to accept financial responsibility for the immigrant being sponsored.

The Hurwitzes (Walter and Frieda) did not plan on going to the United States. Walter liked Europe and wished to remain in Belgium unless forced to leave. But for the Lewys and Westheimers, there was no hesitation. They clung to the hope of a new start in America.

The Lewys were counting on the sponsorship of an American cousin of Werner's who was an attorney in Chicago. My parents hoped to secure an affidavit from some relatives of my father's who had an insurance business in Texas. Although the Tausks (Walter and Hella) were already in New York, they were not yet U.S. citizens and were only permitted to sponsor my grandmother.

Amid the frustration of trying to make these complicated arrangements, the three families managed to get away for a few days at the seashore during the summer of 1939. I recall the beach at Blankenberge being damp and chilly, but looking at photographs taken on the boardwalk gives me a warm feeling about the last time we all gathered together as a family. I recall playing in the sand with my cousins and watching Uncle Werner and Aunt Margot dancing arm in arm on the beach. But my most vivid memory is of strolling along the boardwalk with my parents on either side of me, holding their hands, basking in the warmth and safety that a small child feels when loved and provided for. The world at that moment was a happy place.

In the fall, my parents enrolled me in a public school a few blocks from our apartment. I felt anxious at first, worried that the other children would find out I was German or Jewish. But I had already become fluent in French, so I was able to keep that hidden. And I knew I wouldn't be staying at the school long, because we would soon be leaving for America. I enjoyed meeting other children my age and made friends quickly. I also enjoyed doing schoolwork. I did well on my weekly report card, which pleased my parents. Making them proud of me was the most important thing in my life.

By late in 1939, my parents and the Lewys had finally managed to collect all the necessary papers to secure our visas. While I went off to school clutching my books, my father and Werner left for the immigration office, carrying the precious papers that would enable their families to start a new life in America. Upon arriving there, they were separated and assigned to different lines. Werner's papers were found to be in order and his application was approved. My father's request was denied due to a misspelling of his name in the affidavit sent by his relatives.

It is easy to imagine how, in the confusion of a government office run by officious bureaucrats, two otherwise confident young men would feel powerless to assert themselves. Their lack of fluency in the language no doubt posed a huge obstacle to communication, but the contempt that many Belgians felt toward Germans most certainly played a role as well. For Werner Lewy, being unable to summon the nerve to intervene on my father's behalf came to be the most profound regret in his life. It was a regret that he carried to his grave. On countless occasions in later years, he was given to saying, "If only I had known then what I know now . . . "

But it is unlikely that his protest would have accomplished anything. Trying to reason with the clerks who controlled their destiny would have been as difficult as coming to terms with the cruel quirk of fate by which a single typographical error could spell the difference between life and death. It's a quirk of fate that I may never fully come to terms with and one that I definitely did not understand that day when I got home from school. I only knew that the Lewys were going to America and we were not.

UNITED STATES OF AMERICA
STATE OF ILLINOIS)
COUNTY OF COOK)
CITY OF CHICAGO)

LEE COHN, being first on oath duly sworn, deposes and says that he is an American Citizen by birth; that he was born in the City of Beloit, Rock County and State of Wisconsin; that he is 56 years of age and has continuously resided in the United States of America since his birth. That his present residence is No.1 7217 Ridgeland Avenue, Chicago, Illinois. That he has resided in the State of Illinois for the past 36 years continuously and at the above address for the past 14 years; that he is the head of a family consisting of himself, his wife and two minor children, and resides with the same.

This affiant further states that he is a lawyer by profession, having been admitted to practice law in the State of Illinois in the year 1907 by the Supreme Court of the State of Illinois; that he maintains offices for the practice of law at N. 139 N. Clark Street, Chicago, Illinois.

That this affiant and his wife Miriam R. Cohn are the owners of real estate in the City of Chicago of the value of about $35000.00; that the income from the property is about $4500.00 per annum; that the net income from his business amounts to about $4000.00 per annum; that he carries life insurance in the sum of $6000.00.

That WERNER LEWY, MARGOT LEWY, his wife, and BERNT WOLFGANG LEWY, age 7 years, his son, who are cousins to this affiant on the paternal side, and now resident at No. 99 Chusee de Warve [sic], Brussels, Belgium, desire to come to the home of this affiant at Chicago, Illinois. That this affiant is ready, willing, and able to receive him and his said family and care for them for a period of six months after his arrival and for such a length of time as he and his family may remain, and this affiant guarantees that said Werner Lewy nor his family will become a charge about the Country or the State of Illinois or any subdivision thereof, or until such time as they may be self supporting.

That this affiant is a law abiding citizen of the United States of America and the State of Illinois and bears a good reputation in the community in which he resides; that neither this affiant, nor any member of his family have ever been subject to any criminal or legal prosecution; That for many years this affiant was attorney for the War Veterans Committee of the Chicago Bar Association, and as such had charge of the administering of estates of incompetent, disabled and deceased veterans of the late Worlds; War, and would respectfully refer you to the Chicago Bar Association, 29 S. LaSalle Street, Chicago, Illinois; also to the Honorable Henry Horner, Governor of the State of Illinois, who prior to his election as Governor sat for many years as Judge of the Probate Court of Cook County, Illinois; also the Honorable Ulysses S. Schwartz, Judge of the Superior Court, Cook County, Illinois.

This affidavit is made for the purpose of assisting WERNER LEWY, his wife MARGOT LEWY and minor son BERNT WOLF-

GANG LEWY to come to the home of this affiant at Chicago, Cook County, Illinois, United States of America.

/s/ Lee Cohn

SUBSCRIBED AND SWORN TO BEFORE ME
THIS 16th day of August, A.D. 1939.

/s/_____

Notary Public

By 1939 Jews fleeting Germany were forced to leave their assets behind. BELHICEM was the Belgian organization that financed and otherwise assisted emigration from Nazi Europe.

[Translation]

I, the undersigned, WERNER LEWY (wife and child) acknowledge having received, from BELHICEM, the sum of 16.871,50 Francs for my upcoming voyage from BRUSSELS to NEW YORK, 12/9/1939. I am hereby liable to BELHICEM for the sum of SIXTEEN THOU-SAND, EIGHT HUNDRED SEVENTY ONE 50 FRANCS.

Brussels, December 8, 1939 /s/ Werner Lewy

Name of ship: S.S. PENNLAND
Company: HOLLAND AMERICA LINE
Port and date of embarkation: ANTWERP, 12/9/1939
Port of debarkation: NEW YORK
Subsequent address, if possible:

> LEWY, Werner
> c/o Walter Tausk
> 106 (or) 107, Ford (sic) Washington Ave.
> N.Y., U.S.A.

It was an awkward celebration in December 1939 when the Lewys set off for New York, leaving behind the Westheimers and Mimi, who was still waiting for her own exit number to clear. Mimi was already distraught over being cut off from her relatives in Berlin, and now she was further shaken by the separation from another of her daughters. For my mother and Margot, who were the closest of the sisters, the parting must have been especially painful. As for me, I was jealous of the Lewys' good fortune and angry at my father for what I thought must have been his mistake. I also felt guilty for not being able to hide my feelings better.

I knew that my mother and father also were disappointed, but outwardly they remained optimistic. They believed we would be able to get another affidavit and assured me that we would soon be joining the Lewys in America.

Johanna Boas and Family
December 1939

The Lewy Family
c/o Tausks
New York, N.Y.

My beloved children and dearest Bernilein,

By the time you get this note you will hopefully have landed in good health and fine spirits. I wish you a happy welcome in your new country: may God grant you peace at last. Three days ago we heard that your ship made it safely through all the mined danger zones. What a relief.

We all had other plans for the future, but one must be grateful with things as they are when one sees the dreadful state of affairs in Poland. But you, my dear children, are starting a new life, and God will help you.

Please write about everything, since Westheimers will not be familiar with anything at all. Tell us what they will need and what they should bring. In the hope this finds you all happy, I send you kisses and greetings. One thousand special kisses for Bernilein.

Your loving Mutti and Omi

[postscript to preceding letter]

Dear Lewys,

Wishing you all good things in your new country. Keep up a good attitude and remain hopeful. Everything will surely turn out. My best wishes on your 10th wedding anniversary. We will see each other again on your silver anniversary, the latest!

With my best wishes,
Your brother-in-law, Walter

My dear Lewys,

Hopefully, as you read these few words you already will have landed safely and recuperated from your long voyage. All good things on your 10th wedding anniversary, may you spend the next one in peace. I pray things will work out for us too. In the hope we meet again very soon, I wish you all good things.

Your, Madi

Hopefully the crossing agreed with you and you can spend your anniversary in your new homeland. Much success in the U.S.A.

Best wishes, Julle

All good wishes in your new home.
Friedel

Werner's identification card was stamped with a large "J" as were those of all Jews in Germany. Fingerprints were also required.

On Werner's passport, as on the passport of all Jewish males, the middle name "Israel" was inserted. Jewish females were given the middle name of "Sara."

As the days following the Lewys' departure stretched into weeks and then months, the prospects for a reunion in America became more and more unlikely. Securing an affidavit with my father's name spelled correctly turned out be more than the small hurdle my parents had expected it to be. For reasons that were never clear, my father's relatives were reluctant to send another one, and delays in the mail caused by increasing political tension hampered his efforts to communicate with them.

I was aware of the rising frustration and anxiety in our household, but I busied myself with my schoolwork. I savored the pleasure my parents took from my progress in learning French and the good reports I brought home from school. I believed that by being a good little girl, I could maintain the peace in our house and keep us together and happy. During those impossibly long days as hopes steadily faded, I think my mother's pride in me was the only thing that kept her going.

By May of 1940, the Belgian authorities had begun to round up German men regardless of Jewish refugee status. I recall my parents talking worriedly about people they knew who had been arrested. At this point, it was clear to them that my father's days were numbered.

On May 10, German tanks rolled into Belgium, throwing everyone into a state of panic. When my mother came to get me at school, I could see that she had been crying. She told me the police had come to our apartment and taken my father away. In my mind, he had been arrested and put in jail. My first thought was that he must have done something wrong. My mother assured me that he hadn't, but her explanation confused me—we had been driven from Germany for being Jews, and now my father had been arrested for being German.

My mother got word from her sister Frieda that my Uncle Walter also had been arrested. Frieda and my mother believed that the arrests were only temporary. They had no way of knowing that their husbands were being deported to an international detention camp a thousand kilometers away. When my mother told me that my father would be back home in a day or two, I don't think she was saying that just to reassure me. She believed his absence would be short-lived. Naturally, I believed her.

Recalling the panic and desperation that gripped our home, it is hard for me to reconstruct the events of the next few weeks in an orderly fashion. It is all a flash of fleeting images, some so vivid and terrifying that I still shudder when they come to mind.

Hearing reports that Nazi troops were advancing on Brussels, my mother and Frieda decided to join the thousands of others who were fleeing the city for the rumored safety of the seashore. They were outraged at having had their husbands taken away from them, but mostly, like their two children and elderly mother, they felt lost and frightened.

We packed only a few possessions and left the city on foot. The highways were jammed with cars and trucks and swarms of people. The roads we hiked on were littered with dead horses and menacing-looking soldiers armed with rifles. I remember wanting to look them in the eye, but I didn't dare chance a glance. Tired, hungry, and thirsty, we walked all day, pausing frequently to rest. During bombing raids we took refuge in train cars that sat stalled on the railroad tracks. Sometimes we jumped into ditches with hundreds of other terrified people. At night we slept along the side of the road with clusters of people or in abandoned farmhouses. After eating the small supply of food that Frieda and my mother had brought along, we turned scavenger, helping ourselves to whatever we could find in the kitchens and barns of deserted farms.

When finally we reached the seashore, we learned that the rumors of safety there had been wrong. German troops were already lining the coast. We had no choice but to turn back. I recall being amazed that the beach where we had only recently spent a wonderful family vacation could be transformed into a battleground of war. As we started back in the direction of Brussels, the air raids became more frequent and we often ran terrified for any available shelter.

Perhaps my strongest memory from those few weeks is the sense of relief I felt upon finally getting back home to Brussels. But with German soldiers now occupying the city, life seemed very different and much worse even to a bewildered little girl who had just turned seven years old. My mother did her best to comfort and protect me, but I felt lonely and scared. Without my father on hand, I could see that she was scared too. And she had the added worry of trying to provide for us. With no source of income, she had to turn to the Belgian Jewish Assistance for support. Her French was not good, and she needed my help to fill out what seemed like hundreds of forms. To me it seemed that we spent day after day waiting in line. I often felt ashamed to be taking charity and at the same time guilty for feeling ashamed.

While our life in Brussels was becoming little more than a matter of day-to-day survival, in America, three thousand miles away, the Lewys had moved to Kansas City. After working at a series of menial jobs that did not require fluency in English, Werner had sharpened his language skills enough to find work in the window-display business as a traveling sales-man. Through charm and perseverance, he eventually became very successful, but at that time he was hampered by the obstacles that confront all new immigrants. Aunt Margot did her part, taking in boarders for whom she cooked, cleaned, and did laundry. But the new language was an enormous barrier, and her struggle with it continued for her entire life. She had been accustomed to the comfort of a large, caring family. Now, with her husband on the road much of the time, she found that the new life could be lonely and isolating.

In addition to their own problems, Werner and Margot were worried about us.

Margot Lewy
Kansas City, Missouri
August 17, 1940

Hebrew Immigrant Aid Society
Antwerp, Belgium

I am turning to you in an attempt to get help. My mother, my two sisters with husbands and two children have been living in Brussels since March of 1939. We have not heard from them since the beginning of May. I am so terribly distressed to have heard nothing from my loved ones, and I am hoping you can get some news for me. Has our mail reached them, and our packages with food and clothing? Needless to say, I am indebted to you for your trouble. Thank you for your immediate attention to this urgent request.

National Refugee Service
September 11, 1940

Margot Lewy
Kansas City, Missouri

Your letter of July 23 was sent to us for consideration. We are sorry to inform you that we are in no position to locate your relatives. Our cooperating agencies in Belgium have been unable to function since the invasion. , . .

It appears that it took four months after our frightening trek to the seashore for my grandmother to regain her composure enough to respond to a telegram that the Lewys had sent to us.

Johanna Boas
Brussels, Belgium
September 29, 1940

Margot and Werner Lewy
Kansas City, Missouri

Finally we know where you are! Walter Tausk wrote us that you are not in New York anymore and your move worried me terribly. Thank you so much, dear Werner and Margot, for all your trouble and concern. Your telegram arrived May 12, but we had left that morning and did not receive it until three weeks later upon our return.

We made our way through the fields to and from Ostende and consider ourselves lucky to have found our belongings intact when we returned. We took only one knapsack per person with our most vital belongings and a few blankets. . . . We roamed the countryside subjected to incredible heat. We spent the nights in fields and barns, living off milk and eggs that we found in abandoned farmhouses. All around us there was constant chaos. Everything was a mess but we eventually arrived in Ostende.

But enough of that. It is so sad that the men have received no news from their wives, even though many letters were sent to them. It is all so upsetting. We have only gotten two letters from Walter in the entire four and a half months. Madi has received no mail at all. And we are unable to send money from here. Perhaps you could manage a few dollars from over there. The men have nothing, nothing at all . . . [letter ends here]

Sometime that summer, my mother somehow received word that my father had been taken to a detention camp near the Pyrenees. After an agonizing wait, we finally received a letter from him. I can't recall what my father wrote in his letters, but I remember how much we treasured them. My mother would read and reread each one. We lived from one letter to the next. They helped us cling to the belief that my father would someday return home.

On the same day my grandmother wrote to the Lewys, Walter Hurwitz also wrote them a letter that appears to have been part of a steady correspondence. Although Walter's letter does not refer to the conditions in the camp where he was detained, other accounts make it clear that the camps under the jurisdiction of Vichy France were unspeakably inhumane. Situated in remote areas of the Pyrenees, they were rife with famine and disease.

Walter Hurwitz
Camp des Internes
Saint-Cyprien, Ilot I
Pyrénées-Orientales
France
September 29 1940

Werner and Margot Lewy
Kansas City, Missouri

My dear ones,

Your letter of September 9 arrived a few days before the High Holy Days. You could not have made me happier than by writing me. I thank you from the bottom of my heart for the dollar. I know how difficult it is for you. I also received 100 francs from the Tausks and cannot tell you how much this means to me. On May 10, when I was arrested, I had only 60 francs. I left the rest to Friedel, thinking our separation would be of short duration and she would need it more.

Friedel wrote that she asked you to try to get in touch with my relatives in South Africa. I shall do it from here because I think it best coming from me. Friedel is getting aid through a local community-assistance program. She also is renting a room to Mr. Max Ader, a client of mine who was hiding until now in the town of Hal. He was working as a gardener in a convent until things became too dangerous. Thus it appears that Friedel is managing. Have you received any letters from Brussels? The mail seems so inadequate.

I now feel certain that the possibility of remaining in Europe is out of the question. Until a peace settlement is reached, any exit visa is impossible, and until such a time, it is unlikely I could be reunited with my family to deal with the matter of emigration. Should my own emigration become possible, I would naturally also come to America. But my registration number goes back to 1939, and it will be at least two years before my number is called. I have tried to contact the American consulate, but they were not very helpful. Your efforts to get me an affidavit seem useless at this moment, but your good intentions make me very happy.

I am so glad to see that you, Werner, are doing well enough to be earning $30 a week. Does your territory extend beyond the states of Missouri and Illinois? Of course these states must be quite large and the financial rewards seem fair. If I am ever able to come, I would not go to New York but rather live where you do, in Kansas City. Please write again soon and I wish you all good things for the new year.

With heartfelt wishes,
Walter

There is little doubt that the mail, as Walter stated, was inadequate. But Aunt Frieda, despite having to move to a smaller apartment, was indeed managing—better than Walter imagined and in a way he would not have liked. Frieda had taken in Max Ader as a paying boarder. My grandmother, who had arranged Frieda's marriage to Walter, disapproved of the situation and didn't hesitate to make her feelings known.

As a child, I had no idea what was improper about the relationship between Frieda and Max. I simply knew, from overhearing Mimi and my mother talking, that they both disliked him. But I didn't understand why, because he was very kind to me. Later, when I was old enough to understand what the nature of their relationship had been, I realized that Frieda had been willing to do whatever was necessary for her survival and that of her son. And her relationship with Max turned out to be more than a matter of convenience. Many tragic years later, Max Ader became Frieda's second husband.

For my cousin Henri and me, with our fathers away and the adults around us bickering, it was a chance to become the closest of friends. We were inseparable, taking refuge in our own little world apart from the grownups. During this period and later on, we formed a bond of intimacy that has endured to this day, more than half a century later and across thousands of miles.

The unpleasantness between my grandmother and aunt became so pronounced that it was decided Mimi should stay permanently with my mother and me instead of going back and forth between apartments. We moved frequently. We had to—in order to avoid detection by the authorities. My mother never registered our address, as residents were required to do. As soon as she got word—from a landlord or neighbor—that officials had been asking about tenants in our building, she would make arrangements for us to move. To me, it seemed as if we were packing up our possessions and moving every month. Each time we moved, our new apartment would be smaller, until the three of us lived in two tiny rooms.

I accepted much of the confusion that swirled around us as part of normal life. My mother would forge my father's signature on my weekly report card. I understood implicitly that I should never tell anyone he had been arrested. I understood it would be terrible if anyone—a teacher, a classmate—found out I was a Jew or a German alien. So I told no one.

Despite the pressure of having to be secretive, I loved going to school. I made it my goal to speak perfect French and spent long hours studying. In my mind, not being fluent was the reason my father had been taken away. In retrospect this does not seem like such a naive notion. With a better grasp of the language, my parents probably could have passed for Belgians. I would scold my mother for speaking German, and she would accept my criticism without complaint. But it changed nothing, and I would be exasperated.

My mother spent endless hours at her sewing machine, making beautiful things for me to wear. She would talk about my father and how good it would be again when he returned. She told me about herself as a child, about how she had wanted to be a ballet dancer and had plotted to run away from home and do so. She arranged for me to take weekly dancing lessons and took great pride in watching my progress. These small pleasures provided comfort, making for moments when we were actually happy. But when I had a recital to attend, my mother would have to invent excuses for my father's absence.

We received letters from the Tausks and the Lewys. Although they were having their troubles getting established in America, being able to go there was still our greatest hope. By November it was a faint one, judging by the tone of the letters sent by my mother and Frieda.

Meta Westheimer
Brussels, Belgium
November, 1940

Hella Tausk
New York, N.Y.

[top of letter was missing]

. . . impossible to describe, these seven months have cost us years.
Please do whatever is in your power, because even Mutti deserves a
few more peaceful years of life. Friedel has not yet gotten her visa
either. Please inform the Lewys of this latest news and send them
our love. I thank you from the bottom of my heart for all your trouble and the love you are showing us. I beg you to take care of this as
quickly as possible and don't lose one single day. As soon as you
write us that you have started things moving at your consulate, I will
follow up on my end with both Mutti's and our own visa. But please
get in touch with Julle in France immediately so that you have all
the pertinent facts from his end. Please send your answer via
Switzerland, air mail to Julle's cousin Claire Laden, Eulerstrasse 49,
Basel, and include a forwarding self-addressed envelope. She will
make sure it gets to me. Again, many many thanks.

My loving kisses especially to Florilein,
Meta

P.S. We are getting frequent but depressing news from Uncle
Richard in Berlin.

Frieda Hurwitz
Brussels, Belgium
November 18, 1940

Werner Lewy
Kansas City, Missouri

My dearest ones,

Today I want to write in detail and not just a short note, but
unfortunately we have no happy news. I wish that I could write you

otherwise. Recently I have had mail from Walter via Switzerland, and he has now been transferred to another camp. At least the barracks are air-tight with some electric lights and better drinking water. So far they still do not have straw pallets and are sleeping on the floor. I am only too happy that I gave Walter both travel blankets when he left here. The climate is better, not so damp, but the food is even worse, only watery soup. He is earning a little money on the side making coffee in the canteen, but he writes that it is as good as nothing. When he has no money to buy himself something extra on the side, he, like the others, cannot bear it.

One must also remember the epidemics and sickness that these conditions bring about. It is absolutely incredible, and sometimes I feel incapable and too cowardly to even think about all of this. Above all there is no end to the separation.

There is now a rumor here that America is accepting all affidavits. Walter unfortunately does not have one, and I would be so grateful if you could arrange something for him so that he can get out of this hell before it is too late. There is also the possibility that America would accept people without an affidavit; that would be wonderful, but I am sure it is best to have one. My hands are completely tied here. I know things are hard for you also. You need to prove you can support us, and you barely earn your own daily living. But I don't know who else could help Walter.

I was given permission to send Walter a little money, but it has been three months and I have not received word that he has gotten it. We are able to send some packages now. I can at least send him some underwear, a scarf, and a sweater. At the time of the arrest everyone had to leave "as is." At least I was able to pack a small suitcase for him while the officials were not looking so that he had a few things. But they were all for summer. We had only expected a 48-hour separation and now it has already been six months. It's still completely incomprehensible to me, and just think of what we have lived through in the meantime, and what might yet be coming!

Your,
Frieda

One of the things that increased our sense of desperation around that time was that we suddenly stopped receiving letters from my father.

Eventually my mother learned that he had been stricken with typhoid while attempting an escape to Brussels, but had been recaptured and returned to a camp. I have no idea how she came to be aware of this, just as it is hard to know how much the families in Europe and America knew about anything and when they came to know it. But there is little doubt that one of the primary sources of information for everyone in the family was a relative who was the most physically isolated from the outside world—Walter Hurwitz.

Walter Hurwitz
Camp Gurs
Basses-Pyrénées
France
December 4, 1940

Walter and Hella Tausk
New York, N.Y.

Dear Tausks,

Thank you so much for your letter of November 12. I have not received the package you sent, but that takes two or three months. I know you put it together with love, and hopefully it will get here soon.

Just now I received a note from Julle. I thought he had disappeared. He became ill with typhoid in August and while escaping back to Brussels was hospitalized for two months. At that point he was sent by the French to Camp Agde in the unoccupied zone of France. His barracks is near the city of Montpellier. His address: Camp 3, Baraque 5, Département Herault, France.

I am forwarding all of your letters to him. He writes that he is still very weak. I find it incredible that he was able just to survive. I got a postcard from Meta and she was desperate with worry. At least now we know that Julle is among the living.

The situation with the mail to and from Brussels is terrible. One might get one letter in 12. The French have such a total lack of organization that nothing astonishes me anymore. From Friedel's letters I gather that things are going reasonably well in Brussels. My boy is getting tall and fresh, and he gets his own way with Omi. Friedel writes that she has lost weight, which leads me to believe that food is in short supply.

As you can see from the heading, I have been moved to Camp Gurs, in the foothills of the Pyrénées, some 70 kilometers from Bordeaux. We are about 200 meters higher than before, so it has been quite cold. The barracks are large here. There are 15 blocks, with 1500 people in each block. As we were being moved, scores of Jews arrived from Baden, Germany. They were given 30 minutes to pack a suitcase and allowed to take no more than 2000 francs. Age was of no consequence. Entire nursing homes are gathered here, as well as small children and babies. There are infants in the block across from us with 40 women.

The suffering that exists here makes heaven cry! It is a tragic vision to see women behind barbed wire. Children may be better at adjusting to new circumstances, but I never imagined anything like this. When I see it, I wish from the bottom of my being that our wives will not have to suffer a similar fate. I wrote to Brussels advising them to stay there as long as possible. They might be safe there.

Here, regardless of sex, we are treated the same, separated from one another, in wooden barracks, sleeping on the ground. Few of us have bunks or blankets. Perhaps it is a tiny bit better for the women. In each barracks there is an iron stove that gives off very little heat. Electric lights are scarce. Toilet facilities produce stale water, and all washing is done in filthy so-called bath barracks. Some urinals are installed in both men's and women's barracks. Since it rains almost every day, getting around is very difficult. The ground soaks up water and one sinks into the mud up to the ankles, constantly falling and looking like a pile of shit.

The food is even worse than in the last camp, and that takes some doing. A black liquid passes for coffee in the morning, and for lunch we get watered-down soup. In the evening there are only 200 grams of bread. That is supposedly life-sustaining. Should one try to live on that we would become skeletons, but luckily there is a canteen where we can buy some small items. Without that I shudder to think what life would be like.

Another time I will write more. You cannot appreciate how lucky you are to be safe and together. Hopefully our own women's suffering is almost over. I doubt it, however. Nothing seems to help, one must simply live through it as best one can. With heartfelt wishes and many thanks.

Your brother-in-law, Walter

CHAPTER FOUR | **1941**

By the winter of 1941, we had learned about my father's illness, and my mother was frantically trying to make arrangements for us to join him and go on to the United States. She didn't explain her plans, but what she said made me think we would soon be leaving for America. In reading the letters, I learned that her hope was based on a desperate plea sent to my uncle in New York.

Meta Westheimer
Brussels, Belgium
January 31, 1941

Walter Tausk
New York, N.Y.

My dearest,

I don't know if you have received our many letters, but since the chance arose to send this one air mail via Holland, I am quickly taking advantage of it. Today I only want to write the most important things. First the address: Julius Westheimer, Camp 3, Baraque 5, Rivesaltes, France.

He was in the hospital for three months in Bordeaux, terribly ill with typhoid fever. They sent him back immediately, still in need of convalescing, I'm sure. His quarters consist of filth and hunger. He wrote me that he would love to write you but does not have a penny for postage. Until now he has not been able to contact Walter.

I beg you to send him up to $2 so he might at least be able to write. Also I beg you if at all possible to assist in his freedom, since his health is so poor and the camp is so dreadful. He would need between $50 and $60 to be transferred to better quarters near Marseilles if he can prove probable emigration. He would be able to work on our emigration much better from there, but he needs an affidavit. If our papers were in order, Trixi and I could leave for Marseilles. I beg you, dear Walter, to pay close attention so that no papers are missing. Please send an affidavit immediately to the consulates in Marseilles and Antwerp. Furthermore. please write to the American consulates in Marseilles and Antwerp, and either you or the Lewys write to Houston: Max Westheimer, 305 Shell Building, P.O. Box 353, Houston, Texas, U.S.A.

You must get us a visiting affidavit without delay; I cannot tell you how lonely Julle's letter sounds. He has gone through enough, and I am so grateful to God that he is alive and well again. What I went through without news is over now, but I cannot stand much more. I feel so terrible to have to burden you with all this, but I don't know what else to do. I hope the time will come when we can repay you. Perhaps Werner could also help, but I fear that too much time will be lost in the process.

Mutti's affidavit number is 61627. Rumor has it that the United States has lifted its immigration quota for persons over 60. Mutti would fall in that category. Please find out for me, because her affidavit would have to be renewed and sent to Marseilles and Antwerp also. If we get the temporary affidavit, Mutti will be able to leave with us, because it would be with a heavy heart that I would even consider leaving her behind. And my Julle's life would be easier for 2 or 3 months until our departure. Under no circumstances can I describe what all your efforts mean to us.

Your, Meta

As with so much of the planning that she had to do, my mother's desperate scheme did not work out. A major change came about quite suddenly—probably before Walter Tausk even received her letter.

On a cold night in February, a few months before my eighth birthday, I was awakened by voices in the other room. I could make out my mother, speaking in a hushed tone. The other voice belonged to a man, and though it was familiar, I didn't recognize it right away.

A few moments later, my father came into my room. When he walked to my bed and leaned over me, I recognized him instinctively. But he had so little resemblance to the image I had kept in my mind for the preceding seven months that I had a hard time believing he really was my father. My father was thin to begin with, but the man by my bed was all bones. I can recall thinking, as he leaned in close and hugged me, that he didn't have any skin on his face.

I wasn't surprised to see my father. I had been expecting him to come home, just as my mother kept assuring me he would. But he seemed like a stranger and I was frightened of him. It was a terrible shock to see him so frail.

I learned most of the details about my father's escape that first night when he came back home. He and my mother stayed up late into the morning, and I listened in on their conversation.

At the camp where my father was held after being recaptured, there was a section where corpses were kept before mass burials. Fearful of being recaptured if he attempted to escape, he hid among the corpses for a day. Once he was presumed dead, no one would search for him when he slipped away. Like so many of the prisoners who escaped from the internment camps, he relied on the help of strangers who provided him with rides and shelter on the thousand-kilometer journey back to Brussels.

There was no family celebration to mark the event. Just as the Lewys' departure for America had been spoiled by our having to stay behind, my father's homecoming was a bittersweet reminder to Mimi and Frieda that Walter Hurwitz remained a prisoner. But I was not aware of this, and I did my own celebrating by trying to carry on endless conversations with my father about what had happened in Brussels while he was gone.

Walter Hurwitz
Camp Gurs, France
February 18, 1941

Werner and Margot Lewy
Kansas City, Missouri

My dear Lewys,

Three months have passed since your last letter of October 22. In December I answered. Did you receive the mail? At the end of October, I moved from Saint-Cyprien, and now rumor has it that we will again be put in another camp. There was no advantage to being moved here because we are still kept behind barbed wire. The very worst is to be separated from my family for such a long time. Over 7 months now this ordeal has gone on, and who knows how long it will last?

At present no end to the war is in sight despite the English successes. If we could have waited out the end of the war with our families it would not be so bad. But it is not good for a husband to be separated from his wife. You understand, I'm sure, what I mean. I must be needed at home for financial reasons. Even though I think my family is not in immediate need, it is certain that Friedel has to be very well organized in order to live. I can hardly see how she gets along, considering the difficulty of running a household and managing groceries, including my boy, who needs to go to school a half hour away. Thank God, Omi stands by her side, of that I'm sure.

Here I sit a useless and helpless prisoner. It is a wonder that I have survived thus far. Just when I think that my nerves are shot, I pull myself together, grit my teeth, and start all over again, because I know that in order to survive I must keep my psyche intact. You are surely informed of Julle's bad luck through Meta. He recently was sent to a camp near Perpignan, not far from Saint-Cyprien here. His address is Camp de Rivesaltes, Ilot K, Baraque 16, Rivesaltes. I write him on and off. On the whole he seems improved.

Sadly, I still do not have an affidavit. The American immigration laws are changing and the situation has worsened. Dear Werner, Margot mentioned that you tried to get me an affidavit, and I thank you. I wish you had been successful, even though you know my orientation is toward Europe and I would prefer not to have to leave for America without my family. An affidavit would help get me transferred to the emigration camp in Marseilles, where I would have some freedom to live like a human being again. Just for that I would be so grateful. The process must start in Washington and be forwarded to Marseilles. Please send me photocopies of all your dealings because the American consulate in Marseilles is overworked by Jews from occupied territories hoping to get somewhere via unoccupied France.

There are many people here who know you, Werner. I hope to hear good things, that your business is working out and Berni is doing well in school. I hear that Henri is a fine student and learning very well.

With heartfelt wishes,

Walter

Walter Hurwitz
Camp Gurs, France
March 6, 1941

Walter Tausk
New York, N.Y.

Dear Tausks,

I have just learned about Julle's disappearance from Camp Rivesaltes. I have known for a long time about his great urge to be reunited with Meta and his child, but I feel that this attempted escape will be detrimental to his future emigration. It would have been better to wait and settle his papers to make it possible for his family to join him in the designated camp in Marseilles. This is something I can never consider myself, knowing that all avenues of departure out of Belgium are closed. The last news from Julle was received by a comrade when Julle was in Toulouse, but I have no knowledge whether the undertaking was successful. . . .

Walter

Just as Walter thought it unwise of my father to flee, my father couldn't understand why Walter made no attempt to escape. I recall him talking to my mother about this quite often. I also remember my grandmother being critical of my father's decision and expressing her belief that Walter, her favorite son-in-law, was acting more responsibly by obeying the law. A letter from the Tausks to the Lewys indicates that the issue was a matter of discussion in the United States as well.

Hella and Walter Tausk
New York, N.Y.
March 29, 1941

Werner and Margot Lewy
Kansas City, Missouri

My dear ones,

I have no way of knowing whether Julle did the right thing. I can understand how lonely he was. It is so difficult to know the exact conditions that I do not wish to pass judgment, but after all Julle has a completely different nature from Walter. Hopefully we will continue to get good news and nothing further will happen to Julle.

Now the main question seems to be what will happen to Mutti. I pray we receive news from her very soon.

I send you heartfelt kisses.

Hella

[postscript to preceding letter]

Dear Lewys,

Thank you for forwarding the letters from Mutti, Frieda, and Walter Hurwitz. We were thrilled to get them. On the same day we also received letters of our own that were much like yours. The best news is that Julle is back with his family. It is only too sad that Walter is still away from Frieda.

When I found Meta's letter saying that Julle was already home, I could hardly grasp it. How is it possible that he was able to make this long trip so quickly? What crazy times! What was true one moment is changed the next.

It looks as if everything is falling apart in Europe. Hopefully, Belgium will be spared. I think Mutti might be afraid to make the trip abroad by herself. She could be held up in Lisbon for months waiting for passage. It is a touchy situation, and the fears are well founded on your part. She might be unable to return to Brussels from Lisbon and also unable to enter the United States. We have no way of putting ourselves in their position in today's hellish times, and we have to leave the decisions up to them. I feel terribly sorry for Frieda and hope Walter will soon be released.

Your brother-in-law,

Walter

Perhaps because he was a lawyer, Walter Hurwitz had more confidence than my father in the chance of gaining his release through proper channels. Whatever his reasons for staying in the camp, in retrospect his letters show that he viewed the situation in sadly naive terms.

Walter Hurwitz
Camp Gurs, France
March 20, 1941

Walter Tausk
New York, N.Y.

Dear Walter,

I am now certain that Julle is no longer in Camp Rivesaltes. Two of my letters were returned with a stamp: GONE. I still don't know whether he survived to return to Brussels. I have had no news from Frieda for 6 weeks. The mail from Brussels to here is poor, even if the mail from here seems to be getting there pretty quickly.

Who knows when we will meet again? The separation is so awful, with no end to the war in sight. I dare not think or I would lose my mind. The condition created by separation, the worthlessness placed on human life in prison, the many repeated illnesses, all tax my nerves every step of the way and continually pull me down. I am surprised at how calm and strong I used to consider myself. But I must pull myself together to get through this.

In the next few days Henri will be seven years old. This is the first time I will not be present for his birthday, and I find it most difficult. Hopefully we will leave this camp soon. Conditions here are poor, the climate is very hot in the daytime and extremely cold at night. If one does not dress right, it is easy to get sick. I would write more, but I imagine you know all about the state of affairs from reading the daily newspapers.

Your brother-in-law, Walter

Walter Hurwitz
Camp Gurs, France
March 25, 1941

Werner and Margot Lewy
Kansas City, Missouri

My dear ones,

A few days ago, I wrote you a letter. Just as I was going to mail it, I received a letter from the Tausks with a copy of my affidavit. At the same time, the originals have been sent to Marseilles. You can't imagine my joy or how much this means to me, and I don't know how to ever thank you. The affidavit is first class and so broad that it covers all necessary details, and I will have no problems here.

At last the doors to freedom are opening up for me. I have presented the necessary papers to obtain release from this camp and to enter Camp des Milles, near Marseilles, for emigration. From there it is easy to get a pass to Marseilles or the Côte d'Azur. This will all come about in the next 3 weeks, so please start writing to Camp des Milles, Bouches-du-Rhône, France.

I still can't believe that I will finally be freed from here. In the last two months I have had three attacks of malaria that, though not dangerous, left me terribly weakened due to the tremors and fever. The doctors here make some effort to help. Besides quinine I take shots, but in the end nothing helps. Please do not inform Friedel. I do not want to worry her. I have not heard from her in 4 months, and it is so hard to wait each day for a letter, only to be disappointed. I had suggested several alternative mail routes to her, but none seems to be working.

I would like to know more about your business. Is it worth it for me to learn a trade? Here in the camp I could pick up skills in cooking or baking. As is, I often cook for my comrades. What do you think? When you answer, please let me know if and when you last heard from Frieda, since I am upset about the long silence.

Many thanks again.

Many heartfelt wishes, Walter

In addition to helping Walter Hurwitz, the Lewys were trying to make arrangements to bring my grandmother to the United States and to obtain an affidavit from my father's cousin in Houston. It is easy to imagine the frustration they must have felt about the delays and obstacles they encountered every step of the way.

American Consul
Antwerp, Belgium.

Dear Sir:

I am enclosing affidavit which my wife and I have completed for the immigration of my mother in law JOHANNA BOAS, nee Baruch. (8-15-73). Now residing : Brussels-Uccle, 10 rue des sept bonniers.
I am of course very anxious to have my mother in law here with us, because we have been separated for a long time. Therefore I am ready willing and able to receive her and care for her for lifetime.

I represent a very good house and I am making more than enough to take care of my family, even though my mother in law is added to it.

We have a six room apartment that would be large enough to accomodate at least one more person in a separate room.

I guarantee that said JOHANNA BOAS, nee Baruch, never will become a charge upon the Country or the State of Missouri or any subdivision thereof.

I sincerely hope that my affidavit and supporting documents will be adequate enough so that you are willing to visa the passports of the said JOHANNA BOAS, nee Baruch and permit her to enter the UNITED STATES for permanent residence and to join the petitioner.

The waiting number on the German quota list of Johanna Boas is 61627 (Berlin)

JOHANNA BOAS, nee Baruch has never been active in any political party or will never engage in any subversive activities.

Thanking you, I am very truly yours

Werner Lewy

WERNER LEWY

Subscribed and sworn to before my
April 2, 1941 Ray...
April 2nd, 1941 My Commission Expires Jan. 28, 1943 ...

Werner's affidavit for Mimi. This was the financial support guarantee required by the United States, April 2, 1941.

American Consul
Antwerp, Belgium

Dear Sir:

I am enclosing affidavit which my wife and I have completed for the immigration of my mother in law JOHANNA BOAS, nee Baruch (8-15-75). Now residing: Brussels-Uccle, 10 rue des sept bonniers.

I am of course very anxious to have my mother in law here with us, because we have been separated for a long time. Therefore I am ready, willing and able to receive her and care for her for lifetime.

I represent a very good house and I am making more than enough to take care of my family, even though my mother in law is added to it.

We have a six room apartment that would be large enough to accomodate [sic] at least one more person in a separate room.

I guarantee that said JOHANNA BOAS, nee Baruch, never will become a charge upon the Country or the State of Missouri or any sub-division thereof.

I sincerely hope that my affidavit and supporting documents will be adequate enough so that you are willing to visa the passports of the said JOHANNA BOAS, nee Baruch and permit her to enter the UNITED STATES for permanent residence and to join the petition-ers.

The waiting number on the German quota list of Johanna Boas is 61627 (Berlin).

JOHANNA BOAS, nee Baruch has never been active in any political party or will never engage in any subversive activities.

Thanking you, I am very truly yours

/s/ WERNER LEWY

Subscribed and sworn to before me,
April 2, 1941, Raymond L. Comstock, Notary Public.

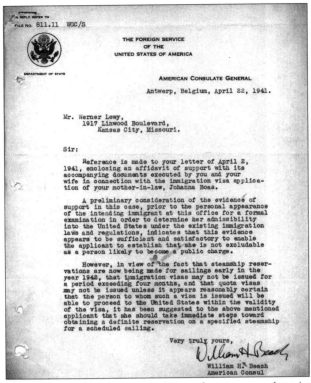

Werner's letter of April 2, received a satisfactory answer from the American Consulate General, April 22, 1941.

The Foreign Service of the United States of America
American Consulate General
Antwerp, Belgium
April 22, 1941

Mr. Werner Lewy
1917 Linwood Boulevard
Kansas City, Missouri

Sir:

Reference is made to your letter of April 2, 1941, enclosing an affidavit of support with its accompanying documents executed by you and your wife in connection with the immigration visa application of your mother-in-law, Johanna Boas.

A preliminary consideration of the evidence of support in this case, prior to the personal appearance of the intending immigrant at this office for a formal examination in order to determine her admissibility into the Untied States under the existing immigration laws and regulations, indicates that this evidence appears to be sufficient and satisfactory to enable the applicant to establish that she is not excludable as a person likely to become a public charge.

However, in view of the fact that steamship reservations are now being made for sailings early in the year 1942, that immigration visas may not be issued for a period exceeding four months, and that quota visas may not be issued unless it appears reasonably certain that the person to whom such a visa is issued will be able to proceed to the United States within the validity of the visa, it has been suggested to the above mentioned applicant that she should take immediate steps toward obtaining a definite reservation on a specific steamship for a scheduled sailing.

Very truly yours,
William H. Beach
American Consul

MAX WESTHEIMER
INSURANCE
309 SHELL BUILDING
PHONE PRESTON 1291
P. O. BOX 355
HOUSTON, TEXAS

May 27th, 1941.

Mrs. Margot Lewy,
1917 Linwood Blvd.,
Kansas City, Mo.

Dear Mrs. Lewy:

Your several airmail letters were received in due course, and your night letter of yesterday was received this morning.

I has been impossible for me to give this matter my attention, as I have not been feeling well lately, and in addition was rushed with work in connection with my business and other matters that demanded immediate attention, in which I had the cooperation of others.

I have spoken to my nephew at various times, and again this morning, and it appears to both of us that no arrangements have been made as to the transportation for the Westheimer family from Brussels to a port, and from there to the United States, and unless such arrangements are made it is entirely useless to arrange for visas for them. If you can give me assurance that tickets will be provided for this family, if and when visas will be issued, my nephew is perfectly willing to issue a new Affidavit.

If you will advise me upon receipt of this letter what you will be able to do in this matter we will give the case further consideration, that is, we will have a new Affidavit issued, if we have the assurance that transportation will be provided in case visas are issued to the Westheimer family.

Awaiting your further advises, I am, with kindest personal regards,

Sincerely yours,

MAX WESTHEIMER.

MW:AG

Letter from Max Westheimer, my father's uncle, to Margot, May, 1941.

Max Westheimer, Insurance
305 Shell Building
Houston, Texas
May 27, 1941

Mrs. Margot Lewy
1917 Linwood Blvd.
Kansas City, Mo.

Dear Mrs. Lewy:

Your several airmail letters were received in due course, and your night letter of yesterday was received this morning.

It has been impossible for me to give this matter my attention, as I have not been feeling well lately, and in addition was rushed with work in connection with my business and other matters that demanded immediate attention, in which I had the cooperation of others.

I have spoken to my nephew at various times, and again this morning, and it appears to both of us that no arrangements have been made as to the transportation for the Westheimer family from Brussels to a port, and from there to the United States, and unless such arrangements are made it is entirely useless to arrange for visas from them. If you can give me assurance that tickets will be provided for this family, if and when visas will be issued, my nephew is perfectly willing to issue a new Affidavit.

If you will advise me upon receipt of this letter what you will be able to do in this matter we will give the case further consideration, that is, we will have a new Affidavit issued, if we have the assurance that transportation will be provided in case visas are issued to the Westheimer family.

Awaiting your further advises, I am, with kindest personal regards.

Sincerely yours,
Max Westheimer

Although the Lewys still had every reason to be worried about us, our life was much improved after my father escaped from the detention camp and returned home. It was very hard at first because he was so sick, and we all lived with the fear that he might be recaptured at any moment. We continued to move to new apartments to avoid discovery by the Belgian authorities, and our prospects for emigrating grew more dim. For me, having my father back home did not always seem like a good thing. It took my mother a long time to nurse him back to health, and this meant that she had less time to spend with me. But by the summertime, when he finally recovered, life seemed almost normal again, better than it had been since we fled Berlin.

Meta and Julle Westheimer
Brussels, Belgium
June 1941

Werner and Margot Lewy
Kansas City, Missouri

My dear ones,

Happy Birthday, dear Wernerlein, all good things, and may the next birthday find all of us together with our darling children by our side.

Mutti's affairs are in order for emigration, she can leave any time. As for us, we have heard nothing new about our situation. Passage might still be arranged, and hopefully will succeed so that we will once more be able to live in quiet and peace. Mutti lives with us now, and we have taken a second room facing the front. Trixi sleeps with Mutti, and the two of them get along famously. I spend the whole day running around with Julle trying to secure passage. When will all of this come to an end?

Trixi is in good health and is a charming child—all but her big mouth! When will we ever be together again? I miss you so terribly. Thank God, Julle is here again, but we have gone through so much. I wish it could be the way it was at home, my dearest sister.

Your ever loving Madi

[postscript to preceding letter]

My dear ones,

We loved reading your letter and can tell that you are already real Americans. In spite of everything, I am so happy to be with my family. I have had no other thoughts since last August. Sadly, my illness took a huge chunk out of our finances, and we have to sacrifice any comforts. At this time emigration is all but impossible. How it will be in the future, no one knows. I am grateful for each hour with Mutti, Madi, and my little sweetheart.

Your Julle

My father steadily regained his strength and eventually managed to find work as a salesman for a food chain. Every day after school, I would wait with my nose glued to the window, wondering what treat he would bring home for me. Aunt Frieda also was managing to survive, relying mostly on Max Ader, who had found a way to eke out a living by selling goods of various kinds on the black market. One thing he sold was cigarettes. When I went to visit Henri, one of our regular amusements was watching Max and Frieda rolling cigarettes by hand. Sometimes Mimi would help them.

Although Mimi constantly reassured me that we would someday get to America, it was clear that she was very sad. It had been almost three years since she had been forced to flee Berlin, and she longed to see her family. She would sit with me for hours reminiscing about her brothers and sisters and fretting about their fate.

Fear of discovery by the authorities forced my parents to move once again, but this time they were able to find a larger apartment with a walled garden and a yard for me to play in. After months of sharing a room with my grandmother, I now had a bedroom all to myself. The only drawback to this new location was that it was farther away from Henri's house, so we weren't able to spend as much time together.

I recall that at our new apartment, my parents were much more at peace with one another. They no longer quarreled. I'm sure this had a lot to do with appreciating each other more after my father's long absence. But in retrospect I realize that there was another factor at work. As time passed, despite the continual flurry of rumors and false hopes, they began to realize that emigration to the United States was no longer possible. While this was a terrible disappointment, they were, at least, no longer caught up in the frustrating process of trying to obtain papers. With their plans and hopes for the future shattered, they resigned themselves to making the most of what they had in the present, taking solace where they could find it.

I was unaware of these complexities, and in many ways it was the best of times. I enjoyed school and my dancing lessons, and basked in the luxury of having two loving parents and a grandmother to dote on me.

Johanna Boas
Meta and Julle Westheimer
Brussels, Belgium
July 15, 1941

Walter and Hella Tausk
New York, N.Y.

Dear children and Florylein,

We received your dear letter and hope that you have received ours. At the moment the topic of emigration is useless. Since you correspond with Walter Hurwitz, you are better informed than we are as to his condition. The postal service here is dreadful. We have received no mail from him. Otherwise we are well. Trixilein has just passed with top marks and is now attending a higher-level school. She takes dancing lessons and is a beautiful, talented little girl. Henri also is very good in school, having come in 8th out of 32 students in his class. On July 7, the Westheimers moved and now have a beautiful apartment with two bedrooms. They were able to get some nice furniture, so that everything looks wonderful and airy with the added luxury of a balcony.

For your birthday, dear Walter, I wish you all good things, health and happiness surrounded by your Hellachen and Florylein. Write soon and enjoy your little doll on your big day.

Your loving
Mutti and Omi

[postscripts to preceding letter]

My dear, dear all,

We were so happy to get your letter. Mutti has written in our place, since we come home very, very tired in the evening. We have a lovely apartment and Mutti feels very much at ease with us. There is a large garden adjoining the house where Trixi can play the whole day and even we are able to spend time in it. So far so good.

I miss you all so much. Nothing new has happened with this emigration business. The consulate has no answers. If only there were no war, so that we could take the next ship to be by your side. Friedel's Walter has sadly not returned home yet. Happy birthday, Walter dear, may all your wishes for next year come true. You will be in our hearts and thoughts. For today I send you all my love,

Your Madi

My dear ones,

I always mean to write in detail, but since I am gone so much, this is all I seem able to do. For your birthday, Walter, I wish you good things. We will share your day in our thoughts, as we frequently share other days. There is nothing new with our affidavits, and we hear nothing from the consulate. With some luck perhaps we can be together at some future date.

Your Julle

While the Lewys' situation was far better than ours, it was clear from the letters we received that for my aunt Margot, life in the United States was very lonely.

Johanna Boas
Brussels, Belgium
October 12, 1941

Werner and Margot Lewy
Kansas City, Missouri

My dearest children and Bernilein,

We received your letters from June, July, and August, and I will try to answer all of your questions, Margotchen. I feel so bad that you miss us so terribly, but believe me, my darling child, I am filled with pain thinking about you also. How nice it was when we could all be together to hear Bernilein laugh heartily. I can hear it still. And how we all sat at the big table with Werner telling his jokes, laughter echoing at every one of his words. And remember, you always used to say to me, "Mutti—laugh!" It all seems such a long time ago and so far away. Will I live to see it all again around me? And should Bernilein be naughty, I would never scold him—I would kiss him.

I am with you in thought every day. I am so glad that you have sent things to Uncle Richard. I especially thank you, Werner, knowing that you have your own brother and sister in Berlin to worry about. You have a big heart, and you will never be sorry to have made me so grateful and happy.

I read your letters over and over, until I get a new one. My only concern is the great distance between us. Friedel is fine, she is managing in spite of Walter's absence. I feel so sorry for him, such a nice man. I hold him in deep regard and feel terrible about his situation. There is also Henri, such a precious child growing up without a father. Trixilein is a sweet child, very good in school.

1000 kisses and loving thoughts from
your Mutti and Omi.

Meta and Julle Westheimer
Brussels, Belgium
October 15, 1941

Werner and Margot Lewy
Kansas City, Missouri

Dear Lewys and Little Berni,

Your letter gave us much pleasure. We too miss you terribly and hope we will meet again. But when might that be? Not for a very long time, I think, and who knows what will happen in the meantime? The main thing is to stay well until then. We are all healthy, but living from day to day.

Friedel is fine, she has no financial worries and seems resigned to the fact that Walter may never return. Perhaps it is better that way. Ader takes marvelous care of her. We too are not short of anything, and if only times were different we would feel quite satisfied. We go to sleep early and have a good friend in the building. I don't work at all anymore and spend the whole day at home. I have been sewing some nice dresses for Trixie and I made her a beautiful coat.

We took some pictures but are unable to mail them to you, so you'll have to be patient. I am happy that Berni is well behaved, since you have to be alone so much of the time, Margot. My dearest, I am sending you all my best wishes for good things. Let us hope that we need not give up on being together again.

Lovingly, Madi

[postscript to preceding letter]

My dear all,

We were so happy to hear that things are going well. We too can't complain, but I think the bad times are just beginning here. Nonetheless, we are grateful for every day that our little family is together. I don't go out much anymore, but that seems to work out too. How is Werner's business? His being gone much of the time can't be wonderful. But one needs to earn one's living as best as one can.

Have you heard anything about my affidavit? For the present it all seems meaningless, but I think about it a lot, and it would be so nice if you could find some means to help us emigrate. Perhaps I'm being too pessimistic and something can still be done from your end. I send you kisses and love.

Your Julle

Although I was not fully aware of it at the time, the letters from my parents indicate that by this point, our living situation had become quite perilous. They wrote in great fear of discovery, deliberately being vague in case their letters fell into the wrong hands. The reason my mother could not send pictures, for example, was because it would call attention to the envelope and the authorities would be able to identify us by making inquiries at the return address. We would "go to sleep early" because of the 8 p.m. curfew that was now imposed on Jews. The "good friend" in our building was our landlady, a kind Belgian Christian on whom we depended for countless favors. I knew even then that she played an important role in our being able to stay in this apartment for almost a full year.

My father did not go out much anymore because he had lost his job and had no chance of finding other work. His usually optimistic tone had changed, for he sensed that our situation, like that of the other Jews in Brussels, would soon get much worse.

Looking back, I find it remarkable that amid the tension and fear created by the ever-tightening restrictions we lived under, I was able to continue going to school. I was well aware that we were in danger whenever we went out and, like my mother, always felt afraid. Outwardly, my father showed no sign of fear. I'm sure that much of this attitude had to do with his wanting to make us feel as secure as possible. But I'm also certain that for him, life in Brussels, however difficult, was a great improvement over living behind barbed wire in an internment camp.

My uncle Walter Hurwitz apparently still thought otherwise. Eight months after he had written to the Lewys about receiving an affidavit and joyously expecting to be transferred, Walter was still in Camp Gurs. When the following letter arrived in New York, the envelope had a blue seal, indicating that it had been opened by the camp authorities, and much of it had been blacked out by the censors.

Walter Hurwitz
Camp Gurs, France
October 31, 1941

Walter Tausk
New York, N.Y.

My dear ones,

Many thanks for your letters, both yours and the Lewys'. I have had no news from Frieda except through you. I can see that you have different opinions about my returning to Brussels. Margot feels that I should go back to Friedel at once and at all costs, while you, Hella, seem to take a more cautious view. I myself am quite undecided, but there are several things I would like to clarify. There are so many problems facing Jews in Nazi-occupied Belgium: the curfew that has been imposed between 8 p.m. and 6 a.m. places all Jews under virtual house arrest, all radios have been confiscated, all ration cards are imprinted with the large red letters Juif, no work permits of any kind, and many other restrictions that make life unbearable.

Twenty thousand Jews have been transported from Germany to Poland. In Paris, Jews are fleeing in great numbers. Should the situation get worse in Belgium, I would ask you to advise Frieda to flee here with my boy. Gurs, bad as it might be, would be far superior to Poland, under the constant watch of the Gestapo. Let her leave all her belongings with her landlord.

All of my friends who have returned to Brussels seem to regret it. Whether Julle did the right thing, I don't know, but I wish to wait it out here a bit longer. After all, I did not escape from Germany only to be sent back there.

In the next few weeks, the political situation should become clear. The most important thing is to stay healthy and withstand the coming winter better than I did the last one. In the suitcase sent to me by Frieda shortly after I got here, there were some warm things. At least we no longer sleep on the floor but on wooden bunks. The barracks are better insulated, and my malaria has let up some. I must only hope to be reunited with my family soon.

Heartfelt wishes, Walter

On December 7, 1941, the Japanese attacked Pearl Harbor. While this event had tragic consequences for thousands of Americans, for my family and other Jews in Brussels it marked the beginning of a period of optimism. When the United States declared war on Germany four days later, my parents believed that the war would soon be over. I remember walking along the street with my father and seeing the huge headlines on the newspapers at the corner newsstand. It was understood that no one dared celebrate openly, but we joined the people gathering in small groups to read the papers. That evening, I had to be quiet while my parents and Mimi tuned in the BBC on our radio, which was now forbidden. They talked excitedly about President Roosevelt and America. Those two words, Roosevelt and America, were synonymous with all things wonderful.

Although I wasn't old enough to understand the details of the news reports, I did understand one basic thing—with America entering the war, the Germans would soon be defeated. To me, this meant we would be able to leave for America in a matter of weeks. And though I can't be certain of it, to this day I believe that my parents had the same expectation.

CHAPTER FIVE **1942**

Despite the oppressive conditions we were living under, we remained relatively happy and hopeful during the first few months of 1942. Mostly this
was due to my parents' continued optimism following the U.S. declaration
of war on Germany. But our life also had some semblance of stability
because we had been able to live in the same apartment on rue de l'Arbre
Bénit for eight months. With the arrival of spring, this was the first time in my
life that I was conscious of being in one place for all of the seasons.

Although I was unaware of the problems involved in sending and receiving mail, it is clear from the letters found in Werner Lewy's closet that getting
mail out of Brussels to the United States had become virtually impossible by
this time. To communicate with the Lewys and the Tausks, my parents and
grandmother were using an intermediary, Max Cohn, a cousin of Mimi's
who had fled to Portugal.

Hella Tausk
New York, N.Y.
February 26, 1942

Margot Lewy
Kansas City, Missouri

Dear Margot,

This morning I received the enclosed letter from Max Cohn,
which I am sending you immediately via air mail. Can you imagine
that, thank God, there is a sign of life from Mutti and, as you will
see for yourself, she is well.

Her letter is dated December 29 and Max wrote his letter on January 11. The whole thing took six weeks getting to us. I must say I felt like a miracle had occurred. For the first time in months I took a deep breath, even though no one knows how long this good news will last. Everything seems to change from one day to another.

I am delighted to hear that the Westheimers have so much pleasure in Trixi, and I can imagine how proud Omi is of her little grandchild, the dancer. At least they have some joy in all of this darkness.

For today there is nothing else. Many good wishes for Berni.

Yours, Hella

It soon became clear that the swift end to the war that we were hoping for would not be forthcoming. My mother and father stopped speaking of Roosevelt and America, and I stopped making plans for crossing the ocean and becoming a movie star. My parents were totally preoccupied with day-to-day survival. The few freedoms we had left were being steadily stripped away, as the Nazis stepped up their efforts to enforce restrictions designed to turn Brussels into a trap for Jews.

We had to live under a curfew, and we did not go out during the evening anymore. We no longer had a radio. One day, noticing that it was not on the mantel, I understood immediately that listening to it was now forbidden.

My parents often learned about new restrictions from notices posted on walls and buildings. They warned me not to stand and read for too long, so that we wouldn't attract attention. At home, my father would tell my mother about rumors of Jews being arrested for violating ordinances. In some cases, neighbors or even fellow Jews had turned them in. My parents would talk about these things late at night when they thought I was asleep. But I would get up and listen in on their conversations from behind my bedroom door. I could tell we were in serious danger, and the fragments of conversation I caught while eavesdropping made me feel frightened and helpless. My father had been taken away from us once before, and I was very conscious that he could be taken away again at any time.

One subject that worried my parents was the behavior of my grandmother. Partly out of defiance, partly out of denial, Mimi came and went almost without fear. She hardly knew any French, and my parents were afraid she might say something in public that would put all of us at risk.

One evening that spring, my mother told me she had to sew a yellow star imprinted "J" on the left lapel of my jacket. The German mandate requiring all Jews over the age of six to wear the "Judenstern" (Jewish star) patch had been enacted months earlier, but until now my parents ignored it. Now conditions had become so oppressive that they felt compelled to comply.

While my mother sewed, I sat beside her watching and feeling humiliated. For me, having to wear the yellow star was the moment when deep fear and misery finally took hold. Until then I had been able to conceal my Jewish identity at school, but now I would be singled out. When I went to school the next morning, I carried my jacket folded in such a way that no one could see the star. Going to school, a place I had loved, now became sheer torture. Each day became a new challenge on how to hide the shameful yellow star. Within a week or so, my parents decided to keep me home. They told me that Jews were being picked up on the streets, identified by their stars.

For the next few months, our apartment became a prison. We stayed home almost all the time, going out only to buy necessities. Although Mimi still sometimes went to stay with Frieda, my parents preferred not to risk the half-hour walk to her apartment, so I didn't get to see my cousin Henri.

Unknown to us, it was around this time that Henri's father, Walter Hurwitz, wrote what was to become his last letter.

Walter Hurwitz
Camp Gurs, France
May 1942

Walter Tausk
New York, N.Y.

My dear Tausks,

It has been many weeks since I have written. Unfortunately your package never did get to me. Packages rarely get lost coming through Portugal, but perhaps someone did not follow your instructions correctly. In April, Friedel wrote that she was doing as well as could be expected. Food is scarce and very expensive, since it must be purchased on the black market. Times are getting worse, and even Julle is complaining!

I often think about my return to Belgium; life in German-occupied territory is becoming increasingly unbearable for Jews. I can't help but feel that Friedel thinks I am safer here than elsewhere. I don't need to hide, and when the door bell rings she need not fear that the Gestapo is coming for me. In spite of everything, I feel torn and wish to be with my wife and child. It has been two years since this war started.

However, here we are mostly optimistic, hoping that the war may come to an end this year. Much depends on you in America, you must quickly send many bombs and pilots. How are you all? Have you suffered from this war? Please write but not too specifically. Also tell me about the Lewys.

There is an official commission here that represents the inmates, and on the whole I feel well. My blood pressure and pulse are normal according to my height. The symptom I mentioned in my last letter, water retention, has improved, so that my health is normal. I was transferred to garden detail; since I have a hernia I only do light work, and my food is improved. Above all I have some structure, and I need that very much. Furthermore we may get an opportunity to leave the camp on passes, but above all I want to go home and hope to be able to rejoin my family by the High Holy Days.

Look for a new address by June 1. Again, many thanks, and my best wishes and kisses to Florylein.

Your brother-in-law and uncle, Walter

After the war, I learned from my aunt Margot that in her letters to Walter, she repeatedly had urged him to try to flee Camp Gurs and return to Brussels. But Walter chose to remain. His fate was decided before the High Holy Days on which he hoped to be reunited with his family. On August 6, 1942, Walter Hurwitz was deported on the first transport to Auschwitz, where he perished. He was forty-eight years old.

Although our situation in Brussels was not as desperate as the one Walter faced in Gurs, the difference was only a matter of degree. We didn't know it at the time, but the summer of 1942 marked the beginning of the blackest period of the Holocaust in Belgium.

In July, the *Association des Juifs en Belgique* (Association of Jews in Belgium), on German orders began distributing call-up notices for "labor mobilization." The deportation of Belgium's Jews now began in earnest. Since many Jews ignored the call-up notices, the Gestapo began a veritable witch-hunt. Nightly raids over the next three months resulted in the arrest and deportation of huge numbers of Jews, especially in Brussels and Antwerp, Belgium's largest cities. This all came alive for me years later when, with my husband and cousin Henri, I visited the little Shoah Museum in Malines, where the detailed portrayal of the notorious "Hundred Days" left nothing to the imagination.

I remember very little of that time, and it was not until after the war that our frequent moves began to make sense to me. My father's refusal to register our names and addresses with the AJB (Association of Belgian Jews) enabled us to remain mobile. Since we could not risk becoming familiar figures in any one neighborhood, my father changed our living arrangements as often as possible. Even though these measures had kept us reasonably safe for a short time, moving was no longer an alternative.

The Belgian underground was very helpful to the country's Jewish populace. As is well documented in Leni Yahil's, *The Holocaust: The Fate of European Jewry, 1932–1945*, the Belgians helped in many ways. In particular, they provided forged documents and hid people, especially children. As I learned much later through conversations with relatives, my parents, along with other Jewish householders, received word through the resistance network that there were many Christians who wanted to save Jewish children. They obtained an address through Alice Ostende.

Meta Westheimer
Brussels, Belgium
July 25, 1942

Margot & Werner Lewy
Kansas City, Missouri

My dearest all, especially little ones,

I hope these lines will reach you, for I want you to know how many serious concerns we now have. Julle and I are not at all well, nor is Friedel, although she doesn't write you often. We are very ill and pray that we will be able to withstand this sickness, since Mutti is no longer young, and what will happen to our darling children?

Trixie only brings us joy, and Henri too is a darling little guy.

We will leave the children's addresses with Kate and Max B. in case Mamilein can't write anymore. After all, we are only human—please make sure that the children come to you. Otherwise there is nothing to write; simply hope that we get well. I feel so sorry for Mutti. If she were with you, so much would be spared her. But nothing can be changed now.

To each and every one of you, I send kisses.

Your Madi

Madi has written you everything. Hopefully everything will soon be better. Many warmest regards to you all,

Julle

Meta Westheimer
Brussels, Belgium
August 10, 1942

Margot and Werner Lewy
Kansas City, Missouri

My dearest all,

I hope you have gotten my mail and read all about Trixi. She and Henri are already gone, and we can only hope that both darling children are healthy. We live in horrible fear and can only hope that things may still blow over. Everything we own is, of course, for our only child, and we give you everything for her upbringing. It is impossible for me to write more about this because my heart is breaking.

Julle has a lot of responsibility. May God only grant that we can endure throughout. Be like a mother to Trixi, because only that thought will permit us to bear such heavy burdens. Naturally we won't take a step without Mutti. Friedel is very independent and gets along well with Ader, who continues to live with her.

Stay well, and God grant that we be reunited one day.

With unending love, Your Madi

ALBUM

My father and me—my mother made my dress with smocking
and lace, especially for this picture.
Berlin, 1938

Westheimers strolling along the boardwalk in Blankenberge, the Summer of 1939

At the beach in Blankenberge, the Summer of 1939
Left to right: Families, Lewy, Westheimer, Hurwitz.

In the back yard of our last apartment in Brussels, 1942

Henri and I loved our pets and our garden. Ottignies, 1943

(*from left*) "Aunt Adèle, Henri, Marriane and me, behind the house in Ottignies, 1943

Behind the rectory, on the day of my First Communion with Father Vaes and Henri, who was a choir boy. Hidden children were frequently converted and brought up Catholic to conceal their Jewish identity and improve their chance for survival. Ottignies, 1943

My grandmother's passport. The middle name "Sara" was imposed on all Jewish females. Passports were stamped with the oversize "J" to identify Jews. At the time, she was still hoping to emigrate to America from Germany.

D

My grandmother vacationing. Baden–Baden, Germany, 1933

My mother in front of my grandfather's publishing house. Berlin, circa 1932

My aunt Frieda and my cousin Henri. It was the custom to have your picture taken while out for a walk. Brussels, 1941

E

My mother fashioned this Hungarian costume for a dance recital. She made it entirely out ot crepe paper. I still remember helping her glue the strips of paper and feeling the excitement of the occasion. December, 1941

Walking down Avenue Louise with my mother. The coat I'm wearing was the last thing she made. My mother rarely used patterns to sew. April, 1942

F

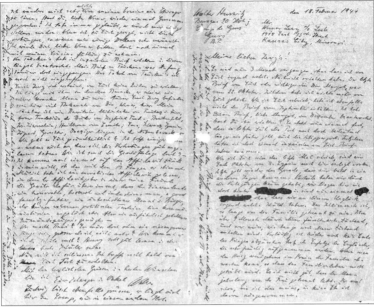

A letter that Walter Hurwitz wrote to Werner in Kansas City, when he was interned at Camp Gurs in France. Mail was mostly censored as shown by the black marks on the page.

Some original entries in my diary, translated in the text.

My grandmother kept a record of the facts surrounding my father's death. Her hand writing became visibly shaken and the facts unclear when she tried to note what little she knew about my mother. I discovered these pages, dated 1943, along with other family records in 1990. (left) Julius Westheimer from Berlin, born in Kannstadt June 13, 1901, was shot to death escaping from Transport XX, Tirlemont, April 19, 1943, age 42. The death certificate was signed by Dr. De Buyst, 68 Avenue de Louvain, Tirlemont. He is buried in the cemetery of Tirlemont, grave #550.

(right) Meta Boas Westheimer, born in Berlin, date and cause of death unknown—in the transit camp of Maline. (She might have meant that she was deported from Maline to a concentration camp)

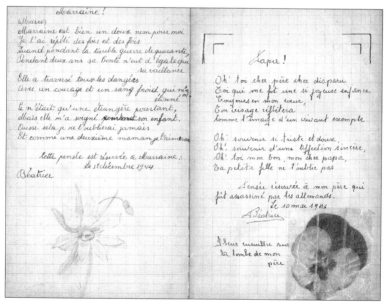

The poem on the left was a tribute to Marraine. The poem on the right was written in memory of my father. The flower I picked from his grave, a pansy, in French is *Pensée*, meaning "thought." This has been symbolic to me of the process of remembrance.

Discovering these two letters, as an adult, turned my world upside down. For the first time in my life, I was able to identify with the panic and despair that my mother must have felt when she made the decision to send me away. Abandoning her only child to an unknown fate was the ultimate sacrifice.

In reading the words that my mother wrote at the time she was living through her personal anguish, I found the mother I had missed so much, so often, at so many crossroads in my life when I looked for answers that might show me how to live. Fifty years after they were written, the words my mother never spoke to me gave my life new meaning.

It is one of the profound regrets of my life that I have no clear recollection of seeing my mother for the last time. But on the day we said goodbye and my father took me and my cousin off to live in the little town of Ottignies, 25 kilometers from Brussels, I had no idea we were parting for the last time. My mother managed to hide her pain from me. She and my father told me that Henri and I would be going to the country for a few weeks.

After being trapped in our apartment for two months, the idea of going on vacation with my cousin seemed like a wonderful adventure.

La Gare du Midi, one of the major train stations in Brussels, was packed with soldiers when we got there. My father seemed very tense, and I was suddenly aware that we were in a very dangerous predicament. The smoke-filled train was crowded with German soldiers, shouting to each other in their native tongue as they walked up and down the aisle. Henri and I knew we shouldn't show any sign that we could understand what they were saying. I tried hard not to even look at them. I focused my thoughts on the doll I had brought along, but Henri was on the verge of tears, and it was hard for me to keep my composure.

My father's discomfort and my sense of danger made the ride seem like an eternity. Many years later, while traveling by train in Belgium, my husband and I sat across from a German man, who made disparaging comments about us to his wife, assuming we were Americans who did not understand him. As I once again pretended not to comprehend, the fear and anger I felt as a child returned. When we got up to leave, I could not refrain from confronting the man in German, and I felt some measure of pleasure in being able to embarrass him. But on that last train ride with my father, I did not have any such satisfaction. Although we looked like the many other Belgian tourists aboard the train, I was terrified that we would be found out.

When we finally reached our destination, the announcement of our stop came suddenly. Henri and I had to scamper to keep up with my father, who was rushing toward the exit. In the confusion, I left behind my doll, which I had been clutching throughout the trip. My father refused to go back for it, and although I didn't cry or even show my disappointment, I was angry at him for a long time.

Outside the station, my father did not seem to know the way. Henri and I followed uncertainly behind him, dragging our small suitcases, which became increasingly heavy as we climbed a long, winding cobblestone road uphill past houses, farms, and fields. The houses we passed were built in an unfamiliar style and all looked alike—two stories, sturdy and bland. Many of the tiny front yards were marked with wooden plaques bearing names. At the top of the hill, we finally came to 18 rue du Ruhaux, the house where we were to stay. The street was at the highest point in the village and overlooked the station below. The name on the plaque in the front yard was *Chez Nous* ("at our house").

We were greeted warmly by two earthy-looking women, older than my parents but younger than my grandmother. The taller one had a cigarette dangling from her lips and her hair tied back in a knot. Like a beloved painting, I can picture her to this day: Jeanne Duchet, the woman I came to call Marraine. Her sister, Adèle, was also kind to me. But she often was away visiting other relatives.

Henri and I explored the house and yard while the adults discussed our living arrangements. I immediately liked the two sisters and wanted to make a good impression. But inside I was scared, knowing that my father would not be staying long. When he kissed me goodbye, he began to cry. I felt baffled and uneasy. This was supposed to be the start of a summer vacation, but seeing my father so sad made it seem like anything but a good thing. I tried to put him out of my mind as soon as he left, but when I fell asleep in my new bed that night, I was still thinking about my father and feeling like I wanted to cry myself.

My worries slowly gave way to curiosity about our new home. Madame Jeanne explained that our last name would be changed to Duchet and villagers would be told we were her nephew and niece. Since she had come to Ottignies from Paris after her husband had died a few years earlier, it was reasonable that we had come from the city to spend the summer in the country with our aunt. She decided we should call her Marraine ("Godmother").

Although having to change identities was a bit confusing, I enjoyed the idea of playing a real game of pretend. I also liked the sound of my new name: Béatrice Duchet. More than anything, I felt a tremendous sense of relief that I would no longer have to wear a yellow star. Despite missing my mother and father, the instant sense of peace and freedom in that small village was a welcome contrast to the tension and confinement of Brussels. With chickens and rabbits in our backyard and sheets flapping on the clothesline, life in Ottignies held the promise of carefree days ahead.

While Henri and I were discovering a whole new world and our loved ones were struggling to survive in Brussels, the letters show that our relatives in the United States were coming to feel more and more helpless.

Walter and Hella Tausk
New York, N.Y.
September 20, 1942

Dear Werner,

Enclosed you will find the letter from Madi. The content is shattering. I wish with all my heart that this dog Hitler might spend months being tortured in the greatest pain, expiring slowly so that he could endure all of the horrors that he is causing thousands of Jews. Hopefully there is still a God in heaven on this Yom Kippur. Like you, I can offer no advice.

A few days ago, I received a note from Margot that sounded desperate. She told me you weren't home for the High Holy Days this year. She sounds so terribly lonely that I think it best that she not be shown the letter. I can well understand the pain of thinking about our dear ones, and knowing my sister, she might be losing her mind over it. On top of everything you are not there to help her bear the pain.

In the last issue of Aufbau I read that all the Jews from Brussels will be sent to a ghetto in Anderlecht. Surely you know the town. I can only imagine the conditions under which they will have to manage, and Mutti at such an advanced age. Our poor dearest ones.

This morning Walter immediately went to HIAS. As I told you on the phone, we want to try to save the children. Perhaps it will be possible to bring them to one of the few remaining neutral countries. I don't know whether it is possible to adopt children, and we won't be citizens until next year. I don't know what to do. Please send us your opinion right away.

With best wishes from your sister-in-law, Hella

Dear Werner,

Hella has written you everything. What our people have to endure is truly horrible. I will see what I can accomplish here, but I have so little hope.

Your brother-in-law, Walter

Walter Tausk
New York, N.Y.
October 4, 1942

Werner Lewy
Kansas City, Missouri

Dear Werner,

We were happy to hear from you. I was wondering about your long silence after our phone conversation and the letter we sent. I have been to the consulate, the Red Cross, and HIAS, but sadly there is no news. Only the German Jewish Children's Aid Society seems interested. I gave them the names of the children and their parents. We can only hope. It's a tragedy what our loved ones have to go through.

Yesterday, through Max Cohn, I received two letters from Mutti and the Westheimers. Even though things are going well enough for us, I have the feeling we are all living on borrowed time. It can't be too long before our new fatherland will call on us to join the army. In Mutti's letter, which unfortunately was dated five months ago, the family seems to think we are already soldiers.

I find it quite puzzling not to have heard anything from Frieda for at least two, if not three years. What do you think is wrong? I hope to hear from you soon.

Your brother-in-law,
Walter

Walter Tausk
New York, N.Y.
October 17, 1942

Werner Lewy
Kansas City, Missouri

Dear Werner,

The letters you enclosed from Friedel and Madi gave us cause for further terrible concern. What our loved ones are living through is simply dreadful.

I'm in complete accord to send a telegram. It should go out immediately to Max Cohn, who might know the exact whereabouts of the children. This week I have been in touch with several organizations. It is impossible to help while the children are in occupied territory. If it is possible to move them to unoccupied France, immediate steps could be taken through the U.S. Committee for the Care of European Children. This group works in conjunction with the Quakers in France. I pray to God they are in unoccupied France. In the last two months, 1200 children have been moved from Belgium to France. Let's hope that our Henri and Trixi are among them.

I'm confused by Meta's letter. What could she mean when she says that Julle has especially difficult responsibilities? Is he with the children, or did he have to take them somewhere? What else could she have meant?

The lot that has befallen our loved ones is too horrendous. I feel so much for the parents and how desperate they must be. How can they stand all this heartache? We can only hope that God will give them the strength to withstand all that the future still holds in store, and that with his help they may someday be together again.

Write me immediately when you send the telegram.

Your brother-in-law, Walter

1942 | CHAPTER FIVE

[Postcript]

My dears,

    I am completely shaken by the letters. I only pray that the children are in unoccupied France. Walter has written everything. Besides, nothing I could write at the moment would make any sense.

Hella

My aunts and uncles in America had every reason to fear the worst for our parents, but Henri and I were more safe and secure and content in Ottignies than they could have imagined. We spent hours roaming the woods neighboring *Chez Nous*, picking currants and mushrooms, and taking turns playing the lead roles in movies we had seen. When we weren't playing, we had chores to do. These also were a great novelty. Each morning we would awaken to the sound of our rooster, and it would be our job to gather freshly laid eggs from the chicken coop. Occasionally one of the birds would have the misfortune of serving as our dinner; this same fate also befell the cutest of rabbits. At a time when the outside world was overrun with unspeakable horror and catastrophe, we had the luxury of wallowing in distaste at the idea of killing for our supper.

I loved my new life with Marraine, but when autumn arrived and we did not pack up to return to Brussels, I began wondering when I would see my mother and father again. They hadn't come to visit all summer, and I hadn't received any letters from them. As the foliage around us changed colors, it brought back memories of Berlin and Sukkot, the Jewish celebration of the harvest. I became very homesick, remembering the time a few years earlier when my father and I had helped build a sukkah (hut) out of branches, leaves, and fruit in the enclave of our synagogue.

Around that time, my father finally did come to visit, but there was no formal observance of the holy days. Although it was wonderful to see him, we had little cause for celebration. I was disappointed that he came alone, and I didn't trust his explanation that my mother had remained behind because it was too dangerous for her to travel. I knew only that I desperately wanted to see her.

My father brought the rest of our clothes and possessions, and I realized that the real purpose of his visit was to work out our continuing living arrangements with Marraine and Adèle. He stayed for only part of one day and seemed very sad and distracted. When it came time for him to leave, he leaned over and picked me up and squeezed me tightly in his arms. He kissed me and whispered in my ear, "*Mon petit bébé*" ("My little baby"). I didn't cry then, but I have cried many times since when I think of that moment, the last time I saw my father. To this day, I can still feel his sense of despair.

I stood in the front yard and watched him walk down the hill, getting smaller and smaller until he finally disappeared from sight. I felt terribly sad as I watched him go, but I was also happy that I would get to stay longer in Ottignies. I felt lucky to have Henri there with me.

Once my father had come and gone, Ottignies was no longer just a vacation spot. Our little fantasy world took on a sense of reality and permanence. Now *Chez Nous* really was our home.

Henri and I began to study the catechism, with the plan being for us to convert to Catholicism and receive our first holy communion. First we had to be baptized. The ritual was performed on October 2 by the village priest, Father Adelin Vaes, in the little church of Saint Joseph. It seemed like a special ceremony because of the sense of secrecy that surrounded it.

Marraine enrolled us at a makeshift school attended by other Jewish children in hiding. The idea of formal education was out of the question, due to the possibility of discovery by the Germans. Our little school had different teachers from day to day. Often we would be taught by a volunteer from the village. The ages of the children ranged from about six to sixteen, and on the rare occasions when everyone attended, there were perhaps eighteen of us in all.

While I was coming to regard Marraine as a caring mother figure, Werner Lewy, the uncle who would become my adoptive father, was thousands of miles away, frantically trying to locate us. It is easy to imagine Werner's frustration as he discovered that the obstacles to his search were not only in Europe but in the United States as well.

THE OFFICE OF CENSORSHIP
THE CABLE AND RADIO CENSOR

IN REPLY REFER TO:
MY/011/21403

67 BROAD STREET
NEW YORK, N.Y.

October 27, 1942.

Mr. Werner Lewy
1917 Linwood Boulevard
Kansas City, Missouri

Dear Mr. Lewy:

It has come to our attention that you have recently filed the following message to Max Cohen, Rua General Querioz Seven RC CALDASDARAINHA, PORTUGAL:

"NEED URGENTLY ADDRESSES OF TRIXIE AND HEIDI TO CONTACT THE COMMITTEES FOR HELP WHERE ARE MOTHER AND SISTERS STOP INQUIRY GERTY BREUER 16 RUE DELECUYER."

Will you please be so kind as to furnish this office with an explanation of the text of this message, including the identity and location of the parties mentioned therein.

Kindly direct your reply to the attention of the Service Division.

Very truly yours,

Andrew W. Cruse
Commander, USNR
Cable and Radio Censor, New York

Correspondence between the Censor's Office in New York and Werner, October 27, 1942

The Office of Censorship
The Cable and Radio Censor
67 Broad Street
New York, N.Y.

Mr. Werner Lewy
1917 Linwood Boulevard
Kansas City, Missouri

Dear Mr. Lewy:

It has come to our attention that you have recently filed the following message to Max Cohen, Rua General Querioz Seven RC CALDASDARAINHA, PORTUGAL:

"NEED URGENTLY ADDRESSES OF TRIXIE AND HEIDI TO

CONTACT THE COMMITTEES FOR HELP WHERE ARE MOTHER AND SISTERS STOP INQUIRE GERTY BREUER 16 RUE DELECUYER."

Will you please be so kind as to furnish this office with an explanation of the text of this message, including the identity and location of the parties mentioned therein.

This is our second letter to you. The first one was mailed on October 27. We shall appreciate your prompt attention to this matter.

Kindly direct your reply to the attention of the Service Division.

Very truly yours,

Andrew W. Cruse
Commander, USNR
Cable and Radio Censor, New York

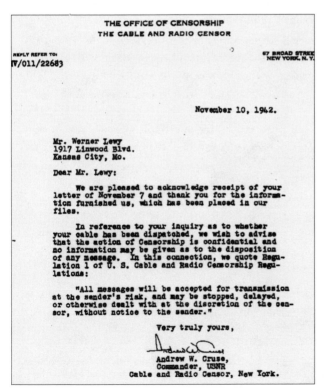

Continuing correspondence from The Office of Censorship to Werner, November 10, 1942.

The Office of Censorship
The Cable and Radio Censor
67 Broad Street
New York, N.Y.

Mr. Werner Lewy
1917 Linwood Blvd.
Kansas City, Mo.

Dear Mr. Lewy:

We are pleased to acknowledge receipt of your letter of November 7 and thank you for the information furnished us, which has been placed in our files.

In reference to your inquiry as to whether your cable has been dispatched, we wish to advise that the action of Censorship is confidential and no information may be given as to the disposition of any message. In this connection, we quote Regulation 1 of U.S. Cable and Radio Censorship Regulations:

"All messages will be accepted for transmission at the sender's risk, and may be stopped, delayed, or otherwise dealt with at the discretion of the censor, without notice to the sender."

Very truly yours, Andrew W. Cruse
Commander, USNR
Cable and Radio Censor, New York

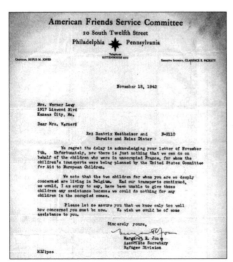

Many letters, just like this one, were sent out daily by the American Friends Service Committee.

American Friends Service Committee
20 South Twelfth Street
Philadelphia, Pennsylvania
November 18, 1942

Mrs. Werner Lewy
1917 Linwood Blvd.
Kansas City, Mo.

Dear Mrs. Werner:

Re: Beatrix and Dieter Hurwitz

We regret the delay in acknowledging your letter of November 7th. Unfortunately, now there is just nothing that we can do on behalf of the children who were in unoccupied France, for whom the children's transports were being planned by the United States Committee for Aid to European Children.

We note that the two children for whom you are so deeply concerned are living in Belgium. Had our transports continued, we would, I am sorry to say, have been unable to give those children any assistance because we could do nothing for any children in the occupied zones.

Please let me assure you that we know only too well how concerned you must be now. We wish we could be of some assistance to you.

Sincerely yours,
Margaret E. Jones
Associate Secretary
Refugee Division

In December 1942, Werner sent a telegram to a cousin in Brussels, Gerty Breuer, by way of the American Red Cross. It did not arrive until almost six months later.

Telegram sent by Lewys to a cousin in Brussels via Red Cross. Mail was unreliable and frequently lost.

Comité International de la Croix-Rouge
Palais du Conseil Général, Geneve (Suisse)
American Red Cross
Washington, D.C.
May 25, 1943

Please give information concerning whereabouts of the two children and rest of the family. Hope you and Maurice are all right. Thanks, and love,

Margot, Werner, Bernt

Like Werner, I too felt desperate for some word from my parents. But I knew that was impossible, and I had made up my mind not to let anyone see how worried I was about them. Near the end of the year, I decided to write them a letter. I did not know at the time that they would never see it. It got as far as my grandmother, who gave it back to me two years later when I returned to Brussels.

> Cher Papy et Mamy,
>
> Je suis encore bien petite,
> Mais je sais déjà bien vous témoigner mon
> affection et mon amour envers vous
> Je sais que pour vous plaire je dois être pour
> commencer bien sage et bien travailler à
> l'école je vous promet que je ferais tous mon
> possible pour bien accomplir cette tâche car
> je sais que vous ne vivez que pour moi je
> vous souhaite une bonne année, et une bonne
> santé j'espère que l'année prochaine à cette heure
> nous pourrons fêter d'année nouvelle ensemble
>   Votre petite fille qui vous souhaite de toute
> son coeur et qui souhaite que nous soyons bientôt
> ensemble
>   Trisi

The last letter that I wrote to my parents, circa December, 1942.

December 1942

Dear Daddy and Mommy,

I am still very little. But I already know how to show you my affection and love. To begin with, to please you, I need to be good and work hard in school. I promise I will do my very best to accomplish this task. I wish you a Happy New Year and good health. I hope that next year at this time we will be able to celebrate the New Year together.

Your little girl loves you with all her heart and wishes that we might soon be together again.

Trixi

CHAPTER SIX

1943

With the arrival of winter, Henri and I began to learn about survival in the country during cold weather. Trips to the backyard outhouse at *Chez Nous* became even more of an adventure now that we had to brave the elements as well as the spiders and other creepy crawlers that lived there. The kitchen, heated by a coal-burning stove, was the only warm room in the house and became the center of our existence.

After being separated from my parents for months, I had come to know Marraine better and better, and I accepted her as the adult in charge. In my mind, she couldn't replace my mother, but I adored her just the same and I loved to watch her work. Tall and slender but slightly stooped, she always wore a simple cotton smock. A kitchen towel hung on her forearm as if it were attached, and a cigarette always dangled from her lips. Her voice was gruff and mildly hoarse, and we knew she meant business on those occasions when she raised it. Although she did not have any children of her own, she was a natural parent in the best sense of the word—firm but fair, disciplining and nurturing us with the commitment of a real mother. To me she just felt good.

Originally from the Lille region in northern France, Marraine had lived in Paris for most of her life. After her husband died, she came to live with her sister in Ottignies. She told us that she had been a nurse during World War I, and that the pain and suffering she had witnessed were the reason she had decided to provide refuge for Jewish children when World War II began.

Under Marraine's watchful eye, we learned many new things that we never would have discovered in Brussels. Three or four times a week, we walked several kilometers to a dairy to get unpasteurized milk, which we drank at room temperature. We learned how to skin the cute little rabbits in our backyard, and they had the misfortune of ending up in a pot of stew.

Marraine was a wonderfully resourceful cook. She could prepare nourishing meals seemingly from nothing, making do with whatever she had on hand. When an unfortunate horse was put to sleep, there would be plenty of meat for us to eat. After a rainfall, she would send us out to gather live snails along the side of the road. These sat in a bowl of flour for a few days until Marraine turned them into a delicacy that we quickly acquired a taste for—escargot.

The villagers in Ottignies viewed Marraine as something of an eccentric, one of the chief reasons being that she was the only person in town with a modern bathtub in her house. It took up an entire little room. Every Saturday evening, Henri and I were sent upstairs to the unheated part of the house where we would shiver through a warm bath. Afterwards Marraine tucked us under the covers of our bed, which she had heated by pressing a black steel iron over the sheets.

Marraine was naturally wary of too much religion, yet leery of none. As part of the plan to keep Henri and me hidden from the Gestapo, our parents had agreed that we should be introduced to the Catholic faith. Marraine understood that they had consented to this for our safety, and she did not attempt to force Catholicism upon us. I'm sure she was surprised by how thoroughly we immersed ourselves in the new religion.

I found real solace in the rituals of the church and worked hard to become the best little Catholic ever. I spent hours practicing my Hail Marys and memorizing all the other prayers. Partaking in the wafer seemed like a special treat, and I considered myself a very lucky child to be allowed to share in this privilege. Deep down, I sometimes felt like I was a traitor to my parents, but being a Catholic seemed safe and peaceful, and I felt no special ties to the Jewish religion.

Perhaps it had something to do with being separated from my own mother, or perhaps it simply fit into my attraction to the world of make-believe, but for whatever reason, as I studied the catechism in preparation for my first holy communion, I became thoroughly infatuated with the Blessed Virgin Mary. I thought about her constantly and prayed to her, asking her to keep my mother and father safe and to reunite me with them soon. I was also fascinated by the idea of confession. I enjoyed the secrecy of kneeling inside the dark confessional and reciting my sins to the priest hidden behind the screen. I liked going to confession so much that I worked at committing misdeeds so I would have sins to confess. A jar of hard candy that Marraine kept in a cabinet in the kitchen offered a wealth of opportunities for sinning and repentance.

In May, a month before my ninth birthday, I made my first communion. Since Henri was not old enough, this was my chance to be center stage. Two other girls from the village participated in the ceremony, but I barely noticed them. I can recall the thrill of anticipation that I felt during the long walk with Henri and Marraine from our house to the church. The sun was shining, and lilies of the valley were in bloom all around us. Marraine had borrowed a white lace dress and veil and nearly new patent-leather shoes for me to wear. The outfit made me think of my mother and the pretty clothes she used to make for me. I felt a little guilty, knowing she would disapprove of the outfit and the ceremony, but I clung to my happy fantasies. Once again, I felt like a little movie star.

After the ceremony Marraine gave me a pocket Bible, which I carried with me and kept under my pillow when I went to sleep. Later that year, we visited a Carmelite convent in the village. I remember looking through a portal down onto a quadrangle where several of the cloistered nuns were working in silence. The serenity of the scene held an enchanting allure for me. After that, during the time I lived in Ottignies, I felt torn between two conflicting ambitions: having a movie career in Hollywood and taking the vows to become a Carmelite nun.

While the life my parents had arranged for me was turning out to be more peaceful and nurturing than they could have hoped for, their own lives were filled with terror. Although I had no way of knowing it at the time, my mother and father were arrested by the Gestapo in February 1943 for violating the curfew. Upon returning to Brussels two years later, I learned from my grandmother that they had been turned in by a Jewish man named Jacques whom everyone feared because he was a known collaborator. They were sent to Caserne Dossin in Malines, near Brussels, a military barracks used as a holding site where Jews were imprisoned before being transported to Auschwitz.

My mother and father were held in Malines for about two months. Around that time, Henri and I were helping Marraine and Adèle plant vegetables in the garden at *Chez Nous*. A full growing season would pass before I learned anything about what had happened to my parents.

In the fall we often worked in a sprawling field near our house, harvesting the leftover corn that was not taken by the farmer who owned the field. I loved competing with Henri to see who could gather the corn faster. One afternoon Marraine told me we had to go to see Father Vaes instead. I was disappointed but didn't say anything, because I knew from her manner that something was very wrong. I felt frightened on the long walk to the church, but I chose not to ask any questions. I instinctively knew that I did not want to hear the answers.

When Father Vaes pulled me onto his lap, my worst fears were confirmed. He told me that Marraine had received terrible news from my grandmother. My parents had been captured by the Nazis sometime ago. When they tried to escape, my father had been shot and killed. My mother had been recaptured, but no one knew where she was.

At first, I refused to believe anything he was telling me. I just wanted him to stop talking, and I was upset that Mimi had not come herself. I wanted to cry, but I couldn't even breathe. I stopped listening and got off his lap as soon as I could.

I can't remember anything about Marraine's actions on our way home. When we got back, I took out a picture of my father and looked at it for what must have been hours. I was too young to understand the finality of death and had never been personally touched by it. Over the next few weeks I took comfort in the belief that my father was now in heaven, where I would surely see him again. I clung to the belief that my mother was all right and that I would see her again soon, especially if I was a good girl.

The limited but devastating details provided by the village priest were the only news received about my parents until my return to Brussels more than a year later. Once my parents were captured, Mimi and Frieda also received little information, but documents found among the letters in Werner Lewy's closet show that my mother made her last contact with them by sending request forms through Madame Alice Ostende, during the summer of 1943. My grandmother never mentioned these precious last requests to me, and

and they came as a sad and shocking revelation of my mother's agonizing pain. By the time I read these forms, it was common knowledge that anything sent to prisoners was kept by the Nazis. The inmates were forced to file request forms in order to obtain luxury goods for this purpose, and also to confuse friends and family into thinking that all their needs aside from a few delicacies were being met.

The food she asked for might have been sent, but no one could have responded to my mother's desperately scribbled plea for one thousand kisses. A few days later, my mother was sent to Auschwitz. She was forty-one years old. I was eleven, and so far away. My father died with my mother at his side, but she died alone, without a loving presence to comfort her.

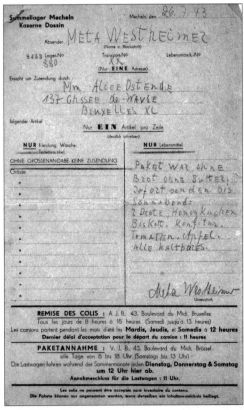

Printed form filled in by my mother urgently requesting food. Sent from Malines to Madame Ostende, July 26, 1943.

Sammellager Mecheln
Kaserne Dossin

Mecheln, den *28. 7. 43*

Absender *META WESTHEIMER*
(Name in Blockschrift)

834
9206
Loger-No *880*

Transport-No *XI*

Lebensmittelk.-No

(Nur **EINE** Adresse)

Ersucht um Zusendung durch :

Mm Alice Ostende
Bruxelles
137 Chssee de Wavre

folgender Artikel :

Nur **EIN** Artikel pro Zeile
(deutlich schreiben)

NUR Kleidung, Wäsche, Toiletteartikel.	**NUR** Lebensmittel.
OHNE GRÖSSENANGABE KEINE ZUSENDUNG	*2 Honigkuchen*
Grösse	*Brot*
Creme - Gesicht,	*Konfitür*
	Tomaten
	billiger Koffer oder
	Korb klein
	Leider Alles zur
	Reise, evtl. Rucksack.
	einige Küsse,

Meta Westheimer
Unterschrift.

REMISE DES COLIS : A. J. B., 43, Boulevard du Midi, Bruxelles
Tous les jours de 8 heures à 18 heures. (Samedi jusqu'à 13 heures)
Les camions partent pendant les mois d'été les **Mardis, Jeudis,** et **Samedis** à **12 heures**
Dernier délai d'acceptation pour le départ du camion : 11 heures

PAKETANNAHME : V. J. B., 43, Boulevard du Midi, Brüssel
alle Tage von 8 bis 18 Uhr (Samstags bis 13 Uhr)
Die Lastwagen fahren während der Sommermonate jeden **Dienstag, Donnerstag & Samstag**
um 12 Uhr hier ab.
Annahmeschluss für die Lastwagen : 11 Uhr.

Les colis ne peuvent être acceptés sans inventaire du contenu.
Die Pakete können nur angenommen werden, wenn denselben ein Inhaltsverzeichnis beiliegt.

Second letter requesting food. Sent from Malines to Madame Ostende, July 28,

Meta Westheimer
Transport # 20
Lager # 880
July 26

Package lacked bread, butter. Send immediately, before Saturday, two breads, spice cake, biscuits, jam, tomatoes, apples, any nonperishables.

Madame Alice Ostende
137 Chaussée de Wavre
Brussels XL
July 28

Please send immediately for trip by Saturday a small inexpensive suitcase.
Spice cake, jam, candy, bread. The last package had no bread and butter. Food that won't spoil for the trip. A thousand kisses.

Around the time my mother was deported to Auschwitz, my uncle Werner Lewy was continuing his relentless efforts to get some word about us. By this time, Werner and Margot had moved from Kansas City to the Hyde Park neighborhood of Chicago. They must have been very worried about the family members still in Europe, because during all of 1943 and 1944, as shown by the absence of any personal letters from this period in Werner's closet, they received no communications of any kind from them.

Index No. _____

A. PERSON(S) SOUGHT

Family name as known abroad	First Name	Sex	M* S	Relationship to No. 1	Date of Birth	Place of Birth
1. Westheimer	Julius	male	M	X X X	6-13-01	Cannstatt/Stuttg. Germany

B. OTHER MEMBERS OF THE FAMILY OR HOUSEHOLD ABROAD *If you are also seeking one or more persons listed below check (✓)*

✓ 2. Westheimer, nee Boas Meta		f.	M	wife	11-9-04	Berlin - German
✓ 3. "	Beatrice	f.	S	student	5-6-33	Berlin - German
☐ 4.						
☐ 5.						
☐ 6.						
☐ 7.						

* MS—Marital Status. Write in: S (single); M (married); W (widowed); D (divorced).   *If you wish to list additional persons, use another blank.*

C. ADDITIONAL IDENTIFYING DATA ON PERSONS LISTED ABOVE

Citizenship*	Religion	Occupation	Last known full address	Country	Date
1. S German	jewish	Salesman	25 rue l'Arbre Benit, Brussels XL, Belgium		'43
2. S German	jewish	wife	" " " "	"	"
3. S German	jewish	student	18 rue du Ruhause, Ottignies, Belgium	"	"
			c/o Mme Pensis.		
4.					
5.					
6.					
7.					

If "Stateless" indicate by "S" and give last citizenship.

D. DETAILS, SOURCE and APPROXIMATE DATE OF LAST NEWS RECEIVED *(If you require additional space use reverse side of this blank)*
(Indicate by number above the person or persons about whom you have the news)

Last News received through American Red Cross Bertie Breuer 16 Rue de L'Ecuyer, Brussels, Belgium, May 29, 1943

E. PERSONS, ADDRESSES and CENTERS OVERSEAS THAT MIGHT BE HELPFUL IN LOCATION *(If you require additional space use reverse side of this blank)*

Name	Address
Mme Bertie Breuer	16 Rue de L'Ecuyer, Brussels, Belg.

F. CLOSE RELATIVES IN THE UNITED STATES OTHER THAN THE PERSON INQUIRING

Name	Address	Relationship to person sought	Check if arrived in U.S. after 1933
Walter Tausk	44 Bennett Ave, New York	Brother in law and uncle	✓

PERSON INQUIRING			
Werner & Margot LEWY nee Boas	5503 Hyde Park Chicago 37 Ill.	Brother in law and sister	

DO NOT WRITE IN THIS SPACE

REFERRING AGENCY _____ FROM CENTRAL EUROPE Inc.
DATE _____

AMERICAN FEDERATION OF JEWS

National Council of Jewish Women. This was the official form filled out when requesting information about missing family members or friends.

In December 1943, more than a year after Werner had sent a telegram through the Red Cross to his cousin Gerty Breuer in Brussels, he finally received notification of a response.

The American Red Cross
 Chicago Chapter
Military and Naval Welfare Service
616 S. Michigan Avenue, Chicago
December 16, 1943

Mr. Werner Lewy
5508 Everett Avenue
Chicago, Illinois

Dear Mr. Lewy:

We have just received through the International Red Cross in Geneva, Switzerland, a short message for you from Gerty Breuer in Belgium.

Inasmuch as this is a personal message, we are interested in having you identify the person who wrote it and would like to deliver the message to you. You may call for this at our office, 616 South Michigan Avenue, between the hours of 9 to 4 from Monday through Friday.

Will you kindly bring this letter with you when you call at our office. If it is impossible for you to come in yourself, you may send some member of your family or telephone the writer at Harrison 5910 to ask that we mail the message.

Very truly yours,
(Mrs.) Alice Loeb

Although he never told me about going to get the telegram, I have no doubt that Werner was waiting outside the office of the Red Cross when it opened the next morning. No matter how shaken he was by the content, I'm certain that he would have immediately noted the date, May 29, and realized that it was very old news, hopelessly out of date.

Reply—Réponse

We had lately little news. Brother in law Westheimer died. Children doing well. His wife very ill. Mama Boas home unknown but in Brussels.

Gerty
29 May 1943

The only solace Werner could have taken from this pitifully brief message was the part about the children doing well. Seven months after the telegram was written, that part was still true. Henri and I were doing very well as we celebrated our second Christmas at *Chez Nous*. I missed my mother and father, and was sad I could not see them, but I was unable to contemplate for very long matters that were outside my day-to-day living situation.

I was totally wrapped up in the customs that came with the observance of a new holiday. Christmas at *Chez Nous* started with hiking out to the woods in search of the perfect tree. My hand-carved wooden shoes provided warmth and cozy protection for my feet. The tree had to be small enough to fit on the little sled we used to transport it back to the house. Marraine chopped it down with a hand axe, letting Henri and me each have a turn. Back at the house, we set the tree up in the living room and spent hours decorating it with tiny white candles. Shortly before midnight on Christmas Eve, we strolled through the village to the little church, with the crisp air nipping at our faces.

CHAPTER SEVEN **1944**

For the first two years Henri and I lived there, Ottignies was an idyllic place. Although we missed our parents and worried about them, we thrived in a rural environment under the care Marraine provided. She felt good about the way she lived, and she had a way of spreading that feeling around. She went to great lengths to create an atmosphere that would be normal for us—at least as she conceived normal life to be for children. She borrowed bicycles that we rode back and forth to school, and she let us play for hours in *Le Bois Papa*, the small forest near our house. With resources so scarce, we had many chores to do for our day-to-day survival, but the overwhelming feeling was one of freedom and discovery.

Much of this simply had to do with being away from Brussels. Despite having to change our names and pose as Marraine's nephew and niece, we no longer lived with the constant fear of being discovered as Jews. Almost everyone in Ottignies knew our secret and the secrets of the other Jewish children hidden there, but no one reported us to the German soldiers who occasionally patrolled the village. Even they seemed friendly, though we were terrified of them and only spoke to them on one occasion when they stopped us on the street and asked our names.

Ottignies was isolated not just from the war, but from the whole outside world. It was a place unto itself, with its own peculiar customs. It was widely known that Father Vaes had a teenaged son—so widely known that even Henri and I were aware of it. I'm sure some villagers disapproved, but most seemed to regard it more with amusement than concern.

By the summer of 1944, even little Ottignies was no longer insulated from the war. On D-Day, with the landing of Allied troops at Normandy, I recall sitting in the kitchen with Marraine and Adèle, listening to news reports on the radio. It was clear that the war would soon be over, and I realized that would mean returning to Brussels. I knew I should be happy that the war was finally ending, but the thought of having to leave Ottignies made me sad. Before that day arrived, though, we still had much to endure. World War II was about to come to Ottignies.

Because of the town's proximity to Brussels, the train station was a strategic military location. Word spread through the village that everyone had to dig underground shelters for protection from Allied bombing, which would be starting up soon. With Henri and me taking turns digging, we spent several days building a shelter in our backyard. When we finished, we had a little underground house stocked with provisions. With an opening covered with tree branches, it seemed more a place to play than a life-saving refuge. Although *Chez Nous* was too far from the station for us to see the train tracks, we had a clear view of the area where relentless bombing was about to take place.

By now, going to our little school was out of the question. German soldiers had begun prowling the streets in earnest, and on two occasions there were reports of them conducting house-to-house searches. Marraine received advance warning, and we had to hide in Le Bois Papa until she came to get us. We never had to stay for more than one night. At first we were frightened, but the forest by then had become our private playground. We had been well schooled about eating for survival, and Marraine made sure we had plenty of provisions. After hiding for a few hours, we came to see the experience as an adventure, a merging of our world of make-believe melodrama and real life. We were a bit disappointed when Marraine came to tell us that it was safe to return home.

After the bombing started, it became a nightly ritual, at once terrifying and thrilling. Some nights, Marraine and Adèle would bring us into their bedroom and let us sleep with them. Most nights, when air raid sirens awakened us, we scrambled for refuge in our shelter. When the all-clear siren sounded and the bombs seemed a safe distance away, Henri and I wandered out into the yard and stood on the crest of the hill, watching the explosions below as if they were part of a spectacular fireworks show. In the daytime, we were free to explore areas where bombs had fallen, crawling into gaping craters, climbing over rubble, and taking care to avoid bomb casings and shell fragments.

One day, while wandering in the woods, we found a parachute. From then on, I was afraid that men jumping out of planes were coming after me. I understood that the town was in the process of being liberated, but the bombing still threatened our safety, and it was hard to keep in mind that the men dropping the bombs were not enemies. I became very scared of the dark and was unable to sleep at night.

For a few days in the fall, the bombing became more intense, continuing on and off throughout the day as well. It stopped suddenly, giving way to an eerie silence. For many hours we were glued to the living room window, looking down the hill. Finally we heard people cheering, and saw a parade of tanks, jeeps, and trucks winding up the road. Villagers began lining the streets to welcome the troops. Marraine ordered Henri and me to stay inside and watch from behind the curtains, but we rushed out to join in the celebration. We stood in awe as the first American tank passed by, but our astonishment was not due merely to the sight of the huge army vehicles. It had to do more with the troops: all of the soldiers who liberated Ottignies were black. Henri and I, like many of the villagers, had never seen a black person. Now there were hundreds of them riding down our street.

Despite the sense of joy that filled the town, the week or so when the Allied troops were in Ottignies was filled with tension. Marraine ordered us to stay indoors, saying we might be hurt during one of the occasional skirmishes with German holdouts. But I suspect her real concern had more to do with limiting our intake of *le chewing gomme*, the evil product the American soldiers were handing out so freely.

The departure of the soldiers was very much like their arrival, with a great deal of fanfare and a seemingly endless, dusty, noisy line of traffic. A feeling of calm settled back over the village. For Henri and me, it also was a time of mixed feelings—we knew that the summer vacation we had gone on two years earlier was nearing an end.

In this little village, my father's death had seemed unreal, and my mother's disappearance, temporary. As long as I was there, it was I, not they, who had gone away. In the two years I had spent in Ottignies, *Chez Nous* had become my home. I didn't want to think about going back to Brussels, and I couldn't bear the idea of leaving Marraine. During the weeks before we left, I began keeping a journal and writing poems. It was a way that I could come to grips with sad, harsh reality. I wrote neatly and was careful not to make mistakes. I wanted to be the perfect, storybook child.

A THOUGHT FOR MY DEAR LITTLE MOTHER

I would like to see her again, even be it for a moment,
My darling little mother,
To see once more her ever-smiling eyes
And her lips so sweet.
To see her again, to be enfolded in her arms.
To hear her tender voice
And to be able to ask so softly,
For the kiss that my heart yearns to feel.

This thought was dedicated to my dear mother: September 16, 1944, at the age of eleven years. Béatrice.

TO THE SOLDIERS OF BELGIUM

I
The soldiers left,
Left their parents, their country,
Left everything to chase the enemy.

II
Their courage carried them
With the single thought
Of combatting the crazed Nazi.

III

What hours spent in anguish yet in pride
When thinking that soon, Belgium,
Their beloved country, would be free.

IV

For those who died as well as those who remain,
O Belgium, one same cry must unite us,
Long live our allies!

These thoughts were dedicated to the soldiers. November 15, 1944. Béatrice.

OH, MY FRANCE!

In spite of having another nationality,
France is my favorite country.
Why? Since it is hard to understand
I will reveal the answer.
From my parents I was separated
By enraged Nazis
Trailing the Jews, their innocent victims.
Everyone filled with fear
Thought, "I might be shot,"
When two women, in spite of the danger to their lives,
Two French women took me in,
Loving me like their own,
Knowing that my father had been killed
And my mother deported,
With only my grandmother remaining.
They spent the time I stayed with them
Completely devoted to me

As though I belonged to them . . .
My mother could hardly love me more,
She whose whereabouts are only known to God,
But in her profound exile She would smile if she knew.
That is my reason for loving France.
May God keep her:
Long Live France.

These thoughts were dedicated to France. November 24, 1944. At the age of eleven years. Béatrice.

MARRAINE!

Marraine is a sweet name to me.
I have said it so many times
When during this terrible World War
For two years her kindness was equaled only by her valor.
She conquered all danger
With a courage and calm that astonished me.
Even though she was a stranger
She cared for me like she would her own child.
And that I will never forget,
For like a second mother I will love her.

This thought is dedicated to Marraine: December 1, 1944. Béatrice.

8:30 P.M. FRIDAY, NOVEMBER 17, 1944

This evening my thoughts go to my dear mommy, who must be lis-
tening to me even in her deepest exile, must know that my heart is
filled with love for her, that I call to her in desperation even though
I know that she is held against her will by a man more powerful in

*every way—the Nazi—but held tight against Marraine's heart I
shed some tears, while a prayer soon brings me comfort and I can
go to sleep knowing that my mother would not be happy if she
thought me sad.*

Béatrice

2:30 SATURDAY, NOVEMBER 18, 1944

*At this moment my thoughts go to my dear lost father, whom death
stroked with its cloak; but how many little girls my age find themselves in the same situation? No one should feel sorry for me; at
Marraine's house I am happy. My father listens to me, sees me, and
follows my every move; he is near me, waits for me in Heaven, where
one day I will join him. I only ask that before I die, I might, like him,
do some good in the world, lead some souls to Heaven . . . that is my
greatest wish from you, my dear papa. And may you also protect
mommy.*

Béatrice

Later that year, my grandmother was able to contact our relatives in
America again.

Johanna Boas
Brussels, Belgium
December 13, 1944

Werner and Margot Lewy
Chicago, Illinois

My dearest children,

At last the day has come when I can write you directly. I hope
you are all well. Trixilein, Henri, Friedel, and I are, thank God, still
here.

We have received no news from Walter in two and a half years.
Dear Julle and my beloved Metachen went to the camp in Malines
two years ago. They were arrested on the street and sent there for
two months, then deported on a transport to an unknown destina-

tion. Like so many others they jumped off the train, but tragically Julle was mortally wounded. My precious Metachen was sent back to Malines, and since then I have had absolutely no news from her. It is all such a tragedy. My poor child, where might she be?

The little ones spent two and half years hidden in the country. They are still there but will come home soon. Trixilein will be with me, and Henrilein with his mother.

Recently a friend of Metachen's contacted me. She has a daughter 10 years old and wants Trixilein to live with her. She owns a villa in the woods and is quite wealthy. She has begged me to agree, since it was Metachen's wish to have Trixilein continue her schooling. She would take piano lessons and participate in many other good things. I know the family and will probably agree to this. It seems best for the child. I would be able to see her every day, and she would be able to visit me. I think I will do this until Metachen returns. These have been such horrible years.

With my love and kisses,
Your Mutti and Omi

Johanna Boas
Brussels, Belgium
December 13, 1944

Walter and Hella Tausk
New York, N.Y.

My dear children,

Today I received a card from Werner and was thrilled to get direct news. Hopefully I will hear from you soon. We are all right, Friedel, Henri, Trixi, and I. We have sadly heard nothing from Metachen or Walter. This disaster is still completely unthinkable. My soul agonizes. I have heard nothing from our whole family in Berlin. I await your news anxiously.

My love and kisses,
Your Mutti and Omi

As the day of our departure for Brussels neared, Henri and I became more and more upset. We wanted to remain Catholic and stay in Ottignies. Once again Marraine took us to see Father Vaes. He told us that our responsibilities for now were to Judaism and our family. When we were older, if we still felt the same way, we could come back. I didn't understand much about responsibilities to Judaism, and I didn't want to look to the future. I made up my mind to enjoy my last few days in Ottignies.

8:30 P.M. DECEMBER 10, 1944

This was a beautiful day and I had a wonderful time at Madame Jacqumotte's house. We celebrated Saint Nicholas Day, and on this lovely Sunday, after much practicing, I danced several times, I played the castanets, and put on a little play, La Cigale et la Fourmi, the moral of which is to render good for evil. Finally the day came to an end after a snack of coffee and cookies. Before going to bed, I thanked the dear Lord for the wonderful day He granted me in His infinite goodness.

Béatrice

8:30 P.M. WEDNESDAY, DECEMBER 13, 1944

After our scout meeting we went for a walk. Being captain, I was in charge of the troop. While walking I felt sad realizing that soon I would have to leave Marraine and my beautiful girl scout troop and return to Brussels. Later we played and I didn't think about it anymore. We had a wonderful time because we played for two hours in the woods. He who does not know the forest and the country does not know the grandest treasure nature has to offer.

Béatrice

Two days before Christmas, Marraine put on her city suit and took Henri and me back to Brussels on the train. It seemed like a lifetime since the trip with my father two years earlier. Henri and I knew how much we would miss Ottignies and Marraine.

Frieda and Mimi were waiting for us at the station. I felt awkward having to appear overjoyed to be back when I was actually unhappy about having to leave the place I had come to know as home. I was happy to see my grandmother and aunt, but with my parents gone, I had no desire to stay in Brussels.

The five of us went to Mimi's one-room apartment on *Chaussée d'Ixelles*, where she had been living alone, dependent on her kindly Christian landlady. The surroundings were completely unfamiliar to me, so I had no sense of "being home." I couldn't imagine living in such a confined place, away from the vast stretches of outdoors that I had come to love so well. Mimi's room was small, and we would have to share a bed. The wash basin and pitcher made me think of Marraine's wonderful bathtub and all the fun we'd had preparing for our baths.

Mimi had gone to a lot of trouble to make my homecoming feel special, but I was miserable. I refused to taste the cookies that she put on the table in front of us. Marraine only stayed a short while, and soon Henri left with his mother to go to the apartment that she still shared with her friend Max. At that moment I felt lonelier than I had at any other time in my life: no mother or father, no Marraine, no Henri. In the two years I had been away, Mimi had become a stranger to me. I knew she would not understand the things I wanted to say. Instead I wrote in my journal.

7:00 P.M. SATURDAY, DECEMBER 23, 1944

Today, after a two-year stay in Ottignies, I was called back to Brussels to my grandmother's side. How great was my sorrow at having to leave my dear Marraine, who overwhelmed me with maternal care. Oh, yes, I loved her and will always love her. I will defend her as I would my own mother. However, I will not cry anymore, because if Marraine knew it would cause her much pain. I will be courageous, that I promise you, Marraine.

Béatrice

CHAPTER EIGHT

1945

The first days back in Brussels were very hard for Henri and me, and even though I had little appreciation for what Mimi and Frieda were going through, the situation was difficult for them as well. After enduring countless hardships brought on by the war, they had to work to win back the hearts of the two children they had not seen for more than two years. And we were no longer the same children. We had thrived in the freedom and relative peacefulness of Ottignies, while they had barely survived in the hand-to-mouth existence of Brussels.

Mimi especially seemed much smaller and shockingly frail to me. Although she never broke down and cried, there was a sadness about her that made it seem as if all her spirit had been drained away.

The war was far from over and resources were scarce, yet Mimi and Frieda went to great lengths to have a Hanukkah celebration at Frieda's that was like a special homecoming for us. As my gift, they had sewn pretty clothes for my doll. But all I wanted was to be back with Marraine at *Chez Nous*, looking at the candles on our Christmas tree.

My grandmother and aunt were startled to discover the devotion to Catholicism that Henri and I had developed. We insisted on going to mass, but they would not permit it. Partly because of this, Henri and I spent most of our time, during our almost daily visits, making plans to run away to Ottignies. We plotted our escape while going for long walks in a park near Frieda's apartment. We were so serious about the idea that we marked out our route on a map that Henri had found in his mother's desk.

For me, living in Mimi's tiny apartment was very depressing and confining. I felt lost in Brussels without my mother, and every day we waited for word from her. Mimi kept assuring me that she would return soon, and I looked for her everywhere. At night I would lie awake, worried that I would-not recognize her if she passed me on the street. After all, I had barely recognized Mimi. I found it impossible to sleep, and I didn't dare move for fear I would wake Mimi up. The bed was filled with bedbugs that left welts all over my body. I could hear the German buzz bombs that were targeted for England. Sometimes they broke down over Brussels, and one of them destroyed a building on our block. I was scared and wanted to go back to Marraine. More than anything, I wanted my mother.

Another thing that upset me terribly when I returned to Brussels was being told by Mimi and Frieda about how my father had been killed and my mother recaptured and taken to an unknown destination. Although they didn't offer much more information than I already had learned from Father Vaes, hearing it from them and being in Brussels made it more real for me. They were so distraught about my mother's disappearance that they seemed to blame my father. I sometimes overheard them saying that my mother might have been back home if it hadn't been for his recklessness in trying to escape. Their criticism of him made me angry, but I didn't say anything about it and I didn't believe it. In my mind, my father was a hero, and nothing anyone said could make me think otherwise.

I was hurt when Mimi told me she was making arrangements for me to live with Flory Szmarag, the sister of one of my mother's friends who had miraculously survived the war. Aunt Flory, as I came to call her, lived in a suburb of Brussels where Frieda and Walter Hurwitz had settled upon first moving from Berlin. Flory's daughter, Ruth, was a year younger than I was, and Flory thought I would be a good companion for her. But I felt unwanted by my grandmother and upset about being far away from Henri.

Excerpts from my diary suggest that I again adapted quickly to the new living situation, but I remember different feelings, which were far more complex. After years of getting by on so little, I liked living in a wealthy household where all of my material wishes were met. Aunt Flory gave me a rabbit coat when I moved there, and I thought it was wonderful. But the diet of rich food made me ill, and the people were strangers. I hoped and prayed every day for my mother to return, and without a nurturing figure like Marraine to stand in for her, I felt very lonely.

8:15 P.M. JANUARY 3, 1945

Today I visited someone in whose home I will be staying as of Tuesday the 8th. I had such a good time, and I owe so many thanks to God for having granted me such a beautiful day, when so many little children do not have anything, not one pleasure, and in spite of my poverty, compared to them, am I not a princess? I met Ruth, who will soon become my sister as well as a 10-year-old boy named George with whom I had a good time, not to forget my first cousin, who was also there. We had a snack, played some more until it was time to go home.

I received a letter from my beloved Marraine and I assure you that it gave me as much pleasure as my visit, and this I mean sincerely.

Béatrice

6:00 P.M. TUESDAY, JANUARY 8, 1945

Today, the 8th of January, I arrived as a new boarder at the house of Madame Szmarag in Woluwé-St.-Lambert. In the evening I felt sad because I was not used to it, but very soon this discomfort passed, and now I feel fine and I thank God to have fallen into such good hands.

Béatrice

6:30 P.M. MONDAY, JANUARY 15, 1945

I have just gotten over a very short illness during which I must say I was treated by Aunt Flory like her own daughter. I was cared for better than a little princess. To them as well as to my dear Marraine I will be forever grateful.

Béatrice

1:00 P.M. MONDAY JANUARY 22, 1945

Today I changed schools. This one as well as the teachers and the students made a pretty good impression on me, even though I do not much like the classes. However, little by little I will get used to them and I will make friends quickly.

Béatrice

As winter wore on, living at Aunt Flory's began to take on a sense of normalcy for me. But I did not develop a feeling of warmth for her that came close to the love I felt for Marraine. Some weekends I went to stay with my grandmother; others, she and Henri visited me. Mimi took us to the movies and had to divide her time between westerns for Henri and musicals or melodramas for me. He and I continued to plot our escape to Ottignies, but I was busy with piano lessons, schoolwork, and making new friends.

8:30 p.m. Sunday, February 18, 1945

What a nice party we organized today, a nice intimate little party with Georges, Ruth, and myself. We put on 12 plays and had the same number of spectators. Also, we organized a club under the name of "Good Humor." Our motto is, "The best for nothing." From time to time we will have little parties with the hope of succeeding in amusing everyone.

Béatrice

6:15 p.m. Wednesday, February 21, 1945

What happiness for me today! Guess who visited me? You'll never know, but my journal will—it was Marraine! We had so many things to tell each other. Marraine spent the night here and tomorrow morning she will leave at 10 o'clock to go have dinner with Henri. I hope that my darling Marraine will come often, and in this hope I sign:

Béatrice

7:45 p.m. Monday, February 26, 1945

Today Ruth had to go to her piano lesson and I asked to accompany her. As soon as I got permission we were on our way. What a trip it turned out to be. First we took the #28 [bus] to get there, and after looking around a little we found it. Then, on the way home, we took the #27 but got distracted and went in the wrong direction. When we were almost at the Bourse [stock market], I asked Ruth if she hadn't noticed that we had gone a different way, and she answered that naturally I was right. We got off and took the #83 on our way home.

Béatrice

Although the war was not yet over, by springtime my relatives in Brussels were corresponding with their loved ones in America again.

Johanna Boas
Brussels, Belgium
April 3, 1945

Werner Lewy
Chicago, Ill.

My dear Wernerlein, Margotchen, and Bernilein,

Your dear letter, the fifth one to date, was received right along with a letter from the Tausks. You need not worry about us, we are healthy and counting on seeing the end of the war soon. That's when we hope to receive news from Metachen and Walter.

Since you ask about Trixilein, let me explain why she is at Flory's house. She has a built-in friend and is able to be with young people who are happy and worry-free. She can feel at home and her every wish comes true. She goes to the theater and to parties. She even attended a dance recital. If it were otherwise, I never would have let her go there.

Friedel, Henri, I have just come home from visiting her, and she looks good. I'm told that I also look good, and I know it is because of your dear letters. At least I know I still have children, even though far away. I constantly read and reread your letters. When I go to bed, I take them and read them until I fall asleep.

Again, my dear ones, do not worry about me. I have a nice airy room overlooking a park. I have nice acquaintances who come to see me. I even go to the movies. After all, we are once again free. In my next letter, I hope to be able to give you news concerning my affi-davit. For now I send you all my best and a thousand kisses.

With heartfelt wishes from your loving,
Mutti and Omi

Frieda Hurwitz
Brussels, Belgium
April 16, 1945

Hella and Walter Tausk
New York, N.Y.

My dear, dear loved ones,

It is unbelievable how excited and filled with pleasure we were to receive your letter, and we hope with all our hearts you will receive our mail very soon.

We suffered a great deal here. Pursued constantly by the Gestapo, we had to live from day to day. Even though we were in hiding, it was necessary to go out for things that we could not rely on other people to get for us. Every time we left, we did not know whether we would see each other again. Day and night, each time the bell rang, we thought it was the Gestapo. It was simply a matter of sheer luck to have survived these times. Our nerves suffered ter-ribly from the constant fear. I am only happy that people over the age of 65 were not arrested. This was lucky for Mutti, who could not be convinced to stay home. It was the worst of times. Thank heav-en it is over, because sometimes I thought I would go crazy. Only the thought of my son held me together. Worries about the children gave me no rest night or day.

On the day of liberation, which came suddenly for us, I heard the first English tanks quite distinctly. I couldn't grasp that I was actually being saved and not caught by the Gestapo. Sadly the Westheimers did not live to see this day. They were picked up on the street by the Gestapo in February of 1943. Julle was shot by German machine-gun fire when he and Madi jumped off a transport in an attempt to escape. He died in Madi's arms. She, tragically, was unable to escape. She was taken to a hospital where the partisans tried to save the Jews. When the attempt failed, she was arrested and brought back to Camp Malines. From there, despite our efforts to get her out, she was deported in July of 1943, and her destination remains unknown. Since then we have heard nothing, but we hope that in spite of the horrors she had to endure, she may still return.

I have not heard from Walter since 1942. He wrote me the day before he was to leave on a transport. Since then no sign of life from him. It has been three years and five months that he has been gone. One cannot write much about this, it hits too deep. You could not understand. Mutti does not yet seem to grasp the horrendous hell that we went through.

Please pass my letter on, I can't write everything in one letter, nor can I write it again.

My special wishes,
Friedel

Frieda Hurwitz
Brussels, Belgium
April 18, 1945

Werner and Margot Lewy
Chicago, Ill.

My very dear ones

It is incredible after so long to once more receive mail from you and be able to write back. Mutti is thrilled with your letters and especially your photographs. Please send more since Mutti hoards them jealously.

My dear ones, what unbelievable luck for you to have been almost the last ship out of here. How happy I am that you succeeded. It would have been unthinkable had you remained in this darkest hell.

The poor, poor Westheimers. I wrote to the Tausks in detail and asked that they share the letter with you, since after all these years there is so much unfortunate news to tell that no one letter would suffice.

My thoughts are running away with me. Mutti is healthy, all things considered. Her eyes and hands seem to be better. She is alert mentally and strong-willed. The one thing that upsets me greatly is how thin she is. Like all of us, she has no fat in her diet. When you send another package, please include butter and cocoa, and you must insist that she eat it, otherwise she will sell it. She has set ideas about needing money of her own for America.

Henri is the image of Walter, build, face, manner, and character. His poor, poor father. It is best not to think too much about it. Trixi is adorable, a beautiful, cuddly child. She has it very good with those people, any wish she has is their command. For Mutti it is impossible to be raising a child again. She no longer has the strength. I think this is a good opportunity for Trixi, and in time she will come to understand it very well. I kiss you with all my heart.

Your Friedel

May of 1945 marked the long-awaited end of the war, as reported triumphantly in my journal. Fifty years later, as I read these lines again, I know that behind the dramatic words there was a very fragile little girl. By then I was coming to realize that the more time passed, the less likely it was that I would ever see my mother again.

7:30 P.M. MAY 8, 1945

Finally, here is the long-awaited day in all of Europe, "Peace." My God, what happiness everyone feels, and what thanks we owe our dear liberators. Neither for me nor for my grandmother is this a true day of peace, and it will come only when my darling mother is able to celebrate with us. But let us unite our hearts in spite of the pain that weighs heavy, let us unite in gratitude for all our friends—the Russians, English, Americans, French, and all our other liberators who have sacrificed their lives for us for our happiness, for our liberty. Gloriously their names will live in history and they will have deserved their glory.

Long live our Allies

Béatrice

6:20 P.M. JUNE 5, 1945

Today I am beside myself with joy, I have turned 12. On this happy day I was very spoiled by everyone with one exception, only this one exception, and it's this one secret that I am going to share with you, my dear journal, confidante of my joys and sorrows, you who surely will never betray me and who will honor my smallest secrets. Well, it's my dearest maman and my dear papa who were not able to share my happiness and my joy. With one smile, one kiss, they could replace the most beautiful gifts in the world, and with this same kiss they could erase my saddest childhood moments. Well, you little journal, you must not be very happy that I only tell you these sad feelings and on such a nice day! But you see, that seems to dominate everything. However, in order to keep you content, I will relate my day to you. There were 12 children, and in the end a photographer came to take our picture. See, nosy, are you content now? I sure hope so, because I plan to sign off, filled with gratitude for Aunt Flory, who was so nice to me.

My first 12-year-old signature
Béatrice
12 years old

By June we still had not received any word about my mother. Many organizations had long lists of survivors, and on my visits to Brussels, I would stand in line for hours with my aunt and grandmother, hoping to get some news. They would also go to the train station, holding placards on which they had printed pleas for information about Meta Westheimer. When we walked the streets of Brussels, I would study the faces of passersby, desperately hoping that someone would turn out to be my mother. Often I would "see" her in the distance, only to become dejected upon discovering, when the woman I had spotted got close, that I was mistaken.

By then we had all heard about the unspeakable atrocities to which Jews had been subjected in the Nazi concentration camps. I had recurrent dreams in which my mother suddenly appeared, walking toward me looking frail and sick but still recognizable. I kept praying and hoping she would return, but I realized that if she had survived, we should have heard something by now. But I never mentioned these thoughts to my grandmother or aunt.

Around this time, the finality of my father's death was also becoming more clear to me. I held fast to my belief that he was at peace in heaven, but my deeper feeling was a desperate wish that he was still alive.

SUNDAY JUNE 18, 1945

A few minutes ago I had my darling father's grave right under my eyes. A wooden cross* with his name engraved on it and a little chrysanthemum plant were the only ornaments on my father's grave. But my aunt and my grandmother arranged some beautiful flowers around it, and we also fixed up the graves of others who, like my father, were real heroes in suffering and glory.

Béatrice

6:00 MONDAY JULY 2, 1945

Today Marraine came to see me. I was so happy to see her again, my dear Marraine. She brought me lots of news; for example, our little cat had an eye poked out . . . poor animal! Marraine promised to return soon, and I hope that she will keep her promise.

Béatrice

Today we started our final exams. I hope to pass them and move on to 6th grade.

By late summer, with mail service almost restored to normal, my relatives were able to carry on a more or less steady correspondence. The Lewys and Tausks frequently sent packages and money in an effort to help us meet our needs.

---

* The original grave was located in Tirlemont where the Belgian underground executed its unique attempts to free the Jews on transport XX. There my father was shot. The Jewish community was not involved in the burials and the crosses remained as markers for Jews and Christians alike. Later the graves were moved to a little town in Holland.

Frieda Hurwitz
Brussels, Belgium
September 7, 1945

Werner and Margot Lewy
Chicago, Illinois

My dear ones,

Again many weeks have passed since I answered your letter. The days go by so quickly that I can hardly handle my daily tasks. It is hard to get housework done since we do not always have gas to burn. We have to burn wood to make dinner. There isn't even any coal. The water is half a flight below me, and the W.C. is two floors below that. You know how primitive the conditions are here.

It is very difficult to get along on ration stamps even if everything has gotten better since the end of the war. You can imagine what your packages mean to Mutti. She probably wrote you that she needs nothing, but that's not true. At the moment I can manage, so please just send all the packages to Mutti.

I'm enclosing a picture of Henri. He is his father, body and soul. Because of the grave sorrows we have suffered here, he is wise beyond his years, my son but already my best friend. Over the Jewish High Holy Days he came to synagogue with me even though he considers himself Catholic. I told him he should come and pray for his poor father and later he could always make up his mind as to what belief suits him best.

The main thing for me is that he become an upstanding, clear-thinking human being, and, thank God, he appears to have all of the prerequisites. You ask what plans I have for my child; how can I answer that when I'm not sure what each day holds for us? He is an outstanding student with all honors, and wishes, so far as he knows now, to become an engineer. It is really a little early to think about all this.

Sadly, Walter cannot be here to see it. I think I will have to give up what small hope remains. Hardly anyone seems to be coming back, just a very few, very young people. It is all so horrendous that one doubts it could be true.

And yet life still goes on. For Rosh Hashanah we were all together for the first time in five years. We even had nudelkuchen.

School won't reopen until the end of October, and even this unnerves me; you see, dear Mahne, I'm just falling apart. Still, I try to feel grateful for each good moment and grab what little luck life grants me.

Kissing you with all my heart, Friedel

Frieda Hurwitz
Brussels, Belgium
October 8, 1945

Hella Tausk
New York, N.Y.

My very dear ones,

Four weeks have gone by without me answering your dear letter, which gave me such pleasure. It always warms my heart when I receive news or a package from you. Sometimes I feel so lonely, especially knowing that Mutti and Trixi will leave Europe soon. I doubly appreciate the letters and knowing that there are loved ones in the world still thinking of me.

In spite of everything, I don't wish to complain, since out of the complete destruction of life I was able to save my child and find a human being who has stood by me through the good and bad of it all. Perhaps things in Europe will improve so that one can build a life again. It is incredibly difficult to get work permits if one did not have them before the war started. We don't know if we can stay here.

My boy, thank God, is strong. He resembles his father in every way, except when he occasionally has a temper tantrum, then he resembles Uncle Ludwig. Where is he now? And all our family from Berlin? One hears nothing from any of them. Last week, we had to report the names of all our deported family members to the Belgian authorities. There will be a search throughout the entire land. It will be the last—then we will be informed whether our dearest ones might still be alive. By the end of the year we should know; there will be lists from all the nearby countries, but there is hardly any hope left for their survival.

Mutti only lives for the day she will go to America. I'm happy for you that you will be together, but I feel sad not to be able to see you even once more. She is already packing and giving much thought to what she needs to take along.

I also hope that things go well with Trixie. She is an adorable child, with a mind of her own! That will only help her to get along in life. Mutti would never have been able to raise her alone. She isn't strict enough. But Trixie is a bright little girl. She will be a beauty; men young and old are already completely taken with her. She is a born movie actress; she sings and dances in an adorable fashion, and of course this was all part of Madi's wish for her.

Poor, poor Madi, Trixi was her whole life! Sometimes I want to scream with pain. We have to shut out our heart and soul in order to deal with the agony of survival. You don't know it; no, you can't grasp the misery that was spared you. You are outside luck itself.

Just think, dear Hella, how you shook and trembled at the thought of your husband being drafted, but even if he had gone into the army, he would have had a chance of returning to you. But anyone who fell into the hands of the Nazis was left without hope. It meant a 99 1/2 percent chance of death. That was why Madi and Julle jumped along with the other Jews. They knew they were being sent to certain destruction and death.

Just now another package has come from you. Henri immediately divided up the chocolate to see how many days he could make it last. He couldn't believe so much chocolate at once. I must stop now or this letter will be too expensive to mail.

1000 kisses to you all,
Friedel

In her letter to the Lewys, Frieda seemed to accept Henri's decision to be a Catholic, but in actuality she was less easygoing about it. Shortly after our return from Ottignies, she began a concerted campaign to discourage our interest in Catholicism. By saving her food stamps, she was able to buy all sorts of treats for us to take on Sunday picnics. We were only permitted to go if we agreed to stop demanding that we be allowed to attend mass. By autumn our faith in the church was starting to weaken, and by year's end our fall from grace was pretty much complete.

Throughout the fall, Frieda was making arrangements for Mimi and me to go to Chicago to live with the Lewys. The day was finally approaching when we would move to America as my parents had planned seven years earlier when we fled Berlin. I was still hoping that my mother would miraculously return, but it is clear from the partial letter that follows that Aunt Frieda had no expectation of seeing her sister again.

Frieda Hurwitz
Brussels, Belgium
December 1945

Margot Lewy
Chicago, Illinois

It is an unspeakable tragedy that Madi did not return. It is too horrible. We saw your ads requesting information, but I doubt that anyone will ever be found again. A good friend of mine came back and told me to give up all hope. So slender a woman as Madi would have been sent straight to the gas chambers, and if not, she would never have been able to endure the conditions and the hunger. My friend only received one slice of bread and two cups of water a day. When she was deported she weighed 74 kilos, and she returned weighing 50 kilos. Her husband and her son were taken from her side, never to be seen again. She simply does not know how she will go on living.

The family with whom Trixie was staying spared nothing for her. She took piano lessons, and they wanted her to attend the best opera and ballet school, but Mutti did not allow it. That seems a shame, since it would have been Madi's wish. Trixie is unbelievably graceful with a beautiful voice. She is a good child but has her father's strong will. Sometimes you can't be sure where you stand with her. She draws hearts straight to her, especially the boys. She will become a beauty one day, and I think that she knows it. You may have some difficulties with her, but not for long, because she always comes around.

The children are going to Ottignies for a few days at Christmas and Trixie will be able to say goodbye. I expect that she and Mutti will leave next month. I'm so happy for Mutti, and Trixie will finally know where she belongs. Mutti makes many mistakes when it comes to raising Trixie. Thank God, she will now go to you; she is a loving, sweet child, in every way beautiful.

Mahne, this child has so many good qualities and the potential to become an outstanding human being. It is just a matter of letting her follow her instincts and talents. She is your child now, you will be her mother forever. You and Werner will do what you deem right, but don't force her to do anything she doesn't want to do. Spoil her a little, she is very feminine. Think of our poor Madi and how sad it is for a child to be without a mother. No matter how wonderful aunts might be, no one can take the place of a mother. Just remember how much Madi idolized her child.

Please don't think I want to take anything away from you, and don't be angry at my writing all this, but I have been close to the child during all these years, and like my son she has become my very own too. She is, after all, our own blood.

[Letter ends here.]

In December I left Aunt Flory's house and returned to Brussels to live with my grandmother. I felt relieved to be with my family again. I knew by now that there was almost no chance of my mother coming back, but being in Brussels made me think there might still be some little hope.

I also felt happy to be able to go to Ottignies with Henri to celebrate Christmas. But this time the ritual of chopping down our little tree, putting it up in the living room, and decorating it with candles was a bittersweet event. From the moment we got there, all I could think about was that I would be seeing Marraine for the last time. Although I was looking forward to going to America at last, I was devastated by the thought of losing another loving, important person in my life.

Resuming life with Mimi, Brussels, circa December 1945.

| **1946**

My last year in Brussels was taken up with the details of leaving for America. I went everywhere with my grandmother because I spoke French and she needed me to get things done. This sudden position of importance turned me into something of a brat. I hated having to speak to Mimi in German and made no attempt to hide my feelings. Moreover, I had grown accustomed to life with Aunt Flory, and Mimi did not have the resources to meet all of my expectations. But she tried.

What little money Mimi had went to make me happy. She spent all of her food stamps to buy me whatever I wanted to eat. On weekends, she took me to see any movie of my choice, and I often chose to sit through it three times in a row. Mimi always packed delicious sandwiches, and we sat for hours in the darkened theater watching Jeanette MacDonald and Nelson Eddy.

I continued to attend school, and getting there required riding by myself on a streetcar, which added to my growing sense of independence. There were many delays leading up to our departure, and at times it seemed as if we would never leave. I thought about nothing but going to America. I filled my head with Walt Disney characters and made my schoolmates envious with stories about Chicago and the American relatives who were sending for me.

8:00 Tuesday March 22, 1946

It's been a long time, my dear confidante, since I have touched your pages with my pen. Oh, my dear, since then many things have hap-

pened, some good, others very sad. First of all, I'm going to America, and if that astonishes you, it is nevertheless true. However, before getting there, there's a whole chapter to relate to you:

Around Christmas my grandmother (who at this moment is crocheting across from me) brought me home from Aunt Flory's house in order to live with her again. Aunt Margot and Uncle Werner have sent us an affidavit which will permit entry to the United States. After doing the necessary errands, Mimi obtained our passport and various papers for the long voyage that will definitely establish us in the United States. Doesn't that feel odd to you, my dear journal? I will no longer write in French but rather in English, and not in our good old Belgium but in America, on the other side of the world. Yes, yes, my friend, that's how it will be, and I will no longer be Mademoiselle but rather Miss Béatrice. At any rate, I think everything will be fine.

Aside from our preparations, other things have also happened; I changed schools in September and I love my new school. At Christmas time I spent five days with Marraine. I also went to the opera for the first time and saw Carmen. It was a marvelous evening. I attended with Aunt Frieda and Uncle Adi and my little cousin (little, hmm! 12 years old) Henri. Well, my dear, now you are informed once more, and I will finish here.

Béatrice

In the final days before our departure, I once again felt torn by conflicting feelings. Although I was eager to get to the enchanted land I had heard so much about, I knew that by going I would be abandoning all hope of seeing my mother again.

Before we left, Mimi and Frieda took me to the cemetery to visit my father's grave once again. Seeing his name imprinted on the wooden cross filled me with sadness.

PAPA!

Oh, dear father, dear one who is gone,
You who filled my childhood with joy.
Always in my heart

Will your face be reflected,
Like a living example.

Oh, memory so sad and sweet.
Oh, memory of sincere affection.
Oh, kind, dear father,
Your little girl will not forget you.

In memory of my father, who was assassinated by the Germans.
May 10, 1946.

Béatrice
(attached is a dried pansy picked from the grave site)

When the day of our departure finally arrived, I felt happy and relieved to be going. I did not allow myself to think about my mother or father or how sad it would be not to be able to see Henri and Marraine. Instead, I dutifully began recording the details of our trip in my journal.

TRAVEL JOURNAL FROM THE SHIP URUGUAY

MAY 25, 1946

6:00 a.m. Finally the day so much awaited; we are leaving for the United States. The bus is here, and after touching farewells, we leave for Le Havre.

6:00 p.m. We've arrived, and before us stands the most enormous and beautiful ship—the Uruguay.

7:00 p.m. We embark. How happy I am! Our ship is not exactly a marvel, but the most important thing is that it will take us to America. Our cabin is hardly the most comfortable. It holds 30 people, but we are making the best of it. There are two dining rooms for 500 people each. Three meals are served: mornings at 7, 8 and 9, lunch at 11, 12, and 1, and evening hours like in the morning.

There are four lecture halls, a party room, and still other rooms. Our ship is quite large; capacity 1000 people. We have just found out that we won't be leaving until Monday at 4 a.m., and in the meantime we will remain aboard.

SUNDAY

I made a very nice friend and we had a wonderful time all day long.

MONDAY

4:00 a.m. Everyone is awake and on deck for departure. I cannot describe my joy!

TUESDAY

Oh, oh. Seasick, seasick. It's totally awful. I'm in a chair on deck all day long.

WEDNESDAY

The weather is very stormy, and I'm so seasick that I want to die.

THURSDAY

Seasick.

FRIDAY

Seasick.

SATURDAY

The sea sickness is finally leaving me a little, and for the first time in three days I'm able to eat breakfast. Afterwards I went for a walk on deck with some friends. We had such a good time and we played tons of tricks on the sailors. After dinner, we went into the party room, where a girl was dancing, and found out that tomorrow there will be a grand going-away party. We spent the evening rehearsing for it.

SUNDAY

America is approaching. Tomorrow at 11:00 we debark. There was a captain's dinner. It was so good that my waiter asked me if I was eating so much to make up for lost time. The afternoon was spent meeting the captain, who described our new homeland to us. After supper, we could sense a feverish atmosphere of excitement. All of the ladies were in evening attire. Everything was very nice, and after 10 o'clock everyone danced. Without tiring I danced until midnight.

MONDAY

We were already up at 4:00 a.m. to see the Statue of Liberty, but we had to wait until 9:00 before seeing the statue that introduced AMERICA, LAND OF THE FREE.

Mimi and I spent two months in New York with the Tausks before going on to Chicago. I was awed by the sheer size of Manhattan, and we went all over the city. I was especially thrilled by the Empire State Building, Radio City Music Hall, and the Statue of Liberty. But understanding that I was with my family wasn't as easy. I barely knew Aunt Hella and Uncle Walter. I was not prepared for the intense heat, the different food, and a new language all around me. I felt lonely and found it hard to pretend I was happy all the time.

At the end of the summer, the Lewys drove out to New York to pick up my grandmother and me. Before going to Chicago, we all spent a few days in the Catskills. I had never seen mountains or a resort, and the only vacation I could remember was the beach at Blankenberge. I was the center of attention when I danced in the amateur night contest. That night, being in America was as wonderful as I had hoped it would be. A few days later, after a car ride that seemed like it would never end, we finally arrived in Chicago, the place I would come to call home.

TUESDAY OCTOBER 7, 1946 AMERICA

Well, my old journal, what do you say? I've been in America four months and, yes, for good. And you know I speak English and just love this language. How do you like it [written in English]?

I'm happy here with my new parents. How sad that my little mother never came back, but I must accept life as it comes, and I think that it presents itself, in spite of everything, in a way that is good for me. I'm having so much fun here and feel surrounded by love.

Do you know that I'm already going to school, and it's superb, because it is so easy, and boys and girls attend together. I even have a boyfriend, and I like him very much. Of course I don't know if he likes me, but if not, I actually wouldn't care.

Tell me, old friend, how does it feel to have an American pen scratch our good old Belgian paper? With all my talking, I forgot to tell you that I live in Chicago now and spent five weeks in New York before coming here. Sometimes I'm really homesick, but it will pass with time, I think.

I received a new journal for Rosh Hashanah, much more beautiful, with a brown leather cover and a lock and key. It has the honor of being American. Jealous, old fellow? You need not be, because I will keep you forever, since you hold a part of my life that I do not wish to forget. And, humble little booklet, you have the most beautiful pages of my life, those of the beginning of my life in America. Don't be afraid, because until January I will still write in French. Afterwards I will keep you as a treasure, and later on, when my hands or those of my children open your pages, they will be a reminder that once upon a time a little girl let her pen wander on these pages. By then you will be an old book, but you will be a reminder to everyone about a very little country far away called Belgium. And now my hands will close you, my hands that are 13 years and 5 months old.

Béatrice Lewy
October 8, 1946, Chicago, U.S.A.

EPILOGUE

Despite the tone of cheerfulness and optimism in the final pages of my journal, the adjustment to living in America was difficult for me. There was the immediate need to learn yet another language, attend yet another school, and make friendships with yet another group of people. As a result of all the sudden changes and shifts I had been forced to face in Europe during the war, I considered myself prepared for these challenges. But I arrived in Chicago with far greater needs, and it took many years before I was finally able to take an inventory of the baggage I brought over with me from Belgium. In fact, I don't think it really happened until I read the letters found in Werner's closet.

To the adults who observed me, I probably seemed remarkably well adjusted. That's certainly how I wanted them to perceive me. I started in eighth grade at the Bret Harte elementary school, where I found the work easy and made new friends quickly. I set my mind on the importance of becoming an American. I wanted to think like an American, look like an American, and sound like an American. Within six months, I had learned English fluently, Midwestern accent and all. I strived to be more American than any of my new American friends. It was no easy task, and I lost myself in the effort. I looked only ahead, seldom back and rarely inside myself. I stopped writing to Henri and Marraine. I focused my attention on becoming the loving adopted daughter of Werner and Margot Lewy. I wanted to be like everyone else—to have a mother and a father, to be part of a family.

I tried very hard not to think about my own mother and father, but at night I had recurring nightmares about passing my mother on a crowded street and not recognizing her. I wanted more than anything to be able to see her again.

119

In my new home, as in so many others, no one spoke about the war years. The subject of survival and the camps was too close and painful. At school I never spoke to anyone about the war, except in idealized terms. No one asked me many questions, and that suited me just fine.

At all levels, my grandmother was having a much harder time adjusting than I was. I tried to help her learn English, but she couldn't manage it much better than she had managed French. For Mimi's benefit, German was the language of choice in our household, but I chose to speak it as little as possible.

By the end of eighth grade, in 1947, I considered America my home. Life in general felt good, though I had some rough moments at home adjusting to the schedule and the rules of a disciplined family household. Despite the restrictions of wartime living conditions, or perhaps because of them, I had been permitted a lot of freedom and flexibility. There was far less of that in my new home, and in many ways I had to learn how to act like a child again. I tried hard to be a perfect one in order to please my aunt and uncle. My grades were excellent and my music teacher selected me to sing the solo at our 8th grade graduation ceremony. I had learned all the popular show tunes and envisioned myself as a future Jane Powell. I was outgoing and made good friends. Catching up for lost time was de rigueur.

At Hyde Park High School, I continued on the same track. In my chosen role as a social butterfly, I sometimes tested the patience of my aunt and uncle, and they created some rough spots for me. In retrospect, I probably had many of the same mixed feelings that most adolescents feel toward their parents, but at the time I resented their efforts to discipline me and often felt that my real parents would have been more indulging. Nevertheless, I gradually came to accept Margot and Werner as naturally as they did me. By mutual agreement and in accordance with my mother's wish, I became Beatrice Lewy at an official adoption ceremony, in 1947.

I attended Sunday School at Congregation Isaiah Israel, in the Hyde Park neighborhood of Chicago and quietly resumed my faith in Judaism. I was confirmed in June 1948 at the age of 15. Father Vaes did well in sending me back to my roots.

During my final year of high school, I received word through my aunt Frieda that Marraine had died. Although by then she had been out of my daily life for more years than I had lived with her, I was still devastated by the news. But coming to grips with America required all my energy and I couldn't stay sad for long.

In 1951, I left Chicago to attend the University of Illinois in Champaign–Urbana. I felt exhilarated by the freedom of finally being on my own. I had been preparing for it a long time, since Ottignies and even before then in many ways. I loved the idea of having my freedom in America, the place where my parents had dreamed of going.

At the university, I met and three years later married, a wonderful man—an American man, Irwin Muchman, the man who is still my husband. Over the years he has come to know me well, but it took a long time for both of us to deal with the part of me that was not always American.

Nevertheless, those were the best of years. Nonstop, without taking a breath, we had two wonderful children, Wendy and Robert (affectionately known as Robbie), two years apart. I loved raising my children, and in many delightful ways I was discovering the meaning of childhood right along with them.

Happily, my grandmother lived to see the birth of my children. A tiny and brave figure to the end, Mimi rarely spoke about what she had lived through during the war. But my mother, who had been her favorite daughter, remained locked in her heart. As we got older, there was a part of me that wanted to ask Mimi many questions about my mother, but I refrained from doing so, not only out of respect for her, but also because I was not ready to deal with any more sadness.

Mimi died in 1960 at the age of eighty-six leaving an unavoidable emptiness in my life. She was my last bridge to my childhood seemingly indestructible during that destructive time. While I was learning what it meant to have my own children and raise a family, Mimi's strength had seemed even more admirable to me.

When my own children were old enough to attend school, I returned to school myself so that I could become a teacher. For more than thirty years, I have been teaching foreign languages, mostly French, and mostly in a classroom setting, though I now do it as a private tutor. Because learning languages was for me a matter of necessity and survival, having the chance to develop the necessary skills and being able to use them to work with children has been and remains an important source of fulfillment in my life.

Through the years, our little family often returned to Brussels and Ottignies, meeting up with Henri and his family. We walked the same roads, crossed the same fields and sat in the same little church. During our visits, Henri and I would reminisce about our years in Ottignies, but it was not until Frieda died about the time the letters were discovered that we were able to discuss some of our deeper feelings and earlier fears.

Our lives took different courses and we lived in distant places, but Henri and I remained close friends. Much because of the enduring bond that we developed as children, our relationship holds special meaning for us both and extends to our mutual families. To his mother's relief, Henri's commitment to Catholicism waned. He became a scientist, and an atheist as well.

Even though my children did not have an opportunity to know their real grandparents, Margot (Gramsie) and Werner (Opa) fulfilled that role with genuine warmth and love. In return, they were adored by their grandchildren. When Margot died in 1979, it was a very sad occasion for all of us, especially Werner, who had been a devoted husband for nearly half a century.

On a beautiful Sunday afternoon in October 1982, I answered a phone call that marked the beginning of the darkest period of my life. Irwin and I were back from a trip to Italy, and Wendy and Robbie drove from Chicago to our home in Flossmoor to welcome us back. After a short visit, they left in Robbie's prized possession, a little Toyota. Within the hour the phone rang. Wendy told me they had been in a car accident. "I'm all right," she said. When I asked about Robbie, she replied, "I don't know." But she feared the worst. A car driven by a drunk driver had jumped the median of the expressway and hit them head on. Miraculously, Wendy was able to walk away. Her brother was killed instantly.

Our beautiful, exuberant son was 24 years old. He was working his way through law school at DePaul University and was about to graduate. The little red Toyota was his graduation present. The entire family was rejoicing in his wedding that was to take place three months later. But in one sudden moment, his life and all its potential came to a tragic end.

For many years, I felt as if my own life had ended. During those pain-filled years, I came to understand in the depth of my soul, the ultimate sacrifice that it must have been for my parents to have parted from me—their only child. I drew strength from the memory of my grandmother who managed to live for my sake, despite her overwhelming burden of sadness and loss. I still had a wonderful husband and daughter—my family—to live for. But I realized that if I chose life, I had work to do. The job is not yet finished—perhaps it never will be.

In 1987 Maxime Steinberg recorded the events that led to my parents' brutal deaths in *La Traque des Juifs*, Volume II, 1942–1944. Although I had heard many of these accounts from members of my family, this was the first time I read a definitive explanation. On the printed page the facts were laid bare.

In February 1943, my mother and father were arrested and sent to *Caserne Dossin* in Malines near Brussels. These were military barracks used as a transit camp where Jews were gathered before being systematically transported to Auschwitz. Within two months—on April 19—my parents were deported on transport XX. The first recorded, deliberate attempt at escape by Jews being deported was planned in Malines and took place on this transport. The escape was incited and assisted by the Jewish and Belgian Resistance who managed to bring the train to a full stop just a few kilometers after its initial formation. My father, Julius Westheimer, #879, was shot and gravely wounded following his flight from the train. He did not die immediately on the railroad tracks as did many others, but with my mother's help he managed to reach the streets of the nearest town—Tirlemont. My mother #880, Meta Westheimer, sick and hurt as well, was able to get my father to the home of a local Doctor De Buy [where he died in indescribable pain]. My mother was then taken to a nearby Catholic hospital for asylum and for treatment. Further research by Mr. Steinberg suggests that the next day the Gestapo engineered a disguised "rescue" leading to my mother's abduction from the hospital and her renewed arrest. She was transported back to Malines and from there deported to Auschwitz—#19, Transport XX, July 31, 1943. My mother was never heard from again.

Reading and translating the letters that were found on a shelf in Werner's closet was a healing process for me. Initially I saw it as an emotional and intellectual challenge, a chance to revisit my childhood through the eyes of cherished and lost members of my family—a way to find a resting place for them. I thought the translated letters would be a lasting gift for my daughter

123

and any children she might have. Wendy and her husband, Sol Rajfer, have a child now—a son, Robert—the new joy of my life.

But the process of working through the letters turned out to be more than a gift for them. It led me on a long personal journey through my own memories. I retraced my childhood every step of the way, and though I often found a sad, bewildered little girl, I also rediscovered the resources that served her well. Finally recording that journey on these pages has been a gift to myself, NEVER TO BE FORGOTTEN.